THE PRACTICE OF PROPHETIC IMAGINATION

THE PRACTICE
OF PROPHETIC IMAGINATION

PREACHING AN EMANCIPATING WORD

WALTER BRUEGGEMANN

Fortress Press
Minneapolis

THE PRACTICE OF PROPHETIC IMAGINATION
Preaching an Empancipating Word

Cover image: © iStockphoto.com/Selahattin BAYRAM
Cover design: Joe Vaughan

Library of Congress Cataloging-in-Publication Data
Brueggemann, Walter.
The practice of prophetic imagination : preaching an emancipating word / Walter Brueggemann.
p. cm.
Includes bibliographical references and index.
ISBN 978-0-8006-9897-3 (alk. paper)
1. Preaching. 2. Imagination—Religious aspects—Christianity. I. Title.
BV4211.3.B775 2012
251—dc23
2011034370

The paper used in this publication meets the minimum requirements of American National Standard for Information Sciences—Permanence of Paper for Printed Library Materials, ANSI Z329.48-1984.

Manufactured in the U.S.A.

16   15   14   13   12   1   2   3   4   5   6   7   8   9   10

Contents

For

Gordon Cosby

Dedication

I am glad to dedicate this book to my old and treasured friend Gordon Cosby, who has lived out his life and ministry in the practice of prophetic imagination. As a wise and durable presence in the Church of the Savior, he has not only talked the prophetic but has walked it day by day in demanding circumstance. His moving spirit, resilient passion, and unfailing resolve have mattered enormously to me, as they have to so many. I celebrate the life and ministry of Gordon and give thanks to God for his faithful, embodied imagination. Along with him, I am glad to celebrate the steadfast ministry of the Church of the Savior with its stubborn, insistent, knowing members.

FOREWORD

ON THE WALL OUTSIDE the door of my study at the Fourth Presbyterian Church of Chicago hangs a framed objet d'art that I see every morning when I arrive at work. What it depicts is not clear at first. There are arrows, streaking lines made with a black Magic Marker, and three prominent phrases—*Orientation, Disorientation, New Orientation*—connected by arrows and underlined several times. Directly beneath these are four more words: *suffering, hope, lament, doubt.* Arrows connect these words and lead to another series of words, at an angle in the bottom corner under the heading *Hymns: crucifixion, resurrection, baptism, dying.* Several asterisks, stars, and exclamation points appear in the margins. The diagram exudes energy and passion, almost electrically charged. It is a single page of Walter Brueggemann's lecture notes on newsprint. Walter was visiting our congregation to preach and lecture and someone had the creative imagination to capture a page of his scribbling, have it framed, and present it to me as a gift.

I like it a lot. It reminds me of the man, his energy, his passion for truth-telling, and his extraordinary and accessible biblical scholarship. These are the sources of his fearless commitment to social justice, his love for the theological tradition and its ageless themes of sin, grace, forgiveness, and restoration, and most remarkably, his confidence in the church as the place where transformative good news is proclaimed and heard. On occasion, academics have been known to be dismissive of the church—"institutional religion"—as irrelevant, hopelessly mundane, and sometimes toxic. Not Walter Brueggemann. In the pages that follow, and consistently throughout his scholarly work, there is a wise sensitivity to the realities of the church and an effort to be helpful, to make common cause with those of us who presume to stand in pulpits on Sunday morning and say something faithful. I am grateful to him and for him, and I smile every morning as his energetic scribbling helps me launch another day of ministry.

I was honored to be invited by Walter to write a foreword for *The Practice of Prophetic Imagination*. I assumed I could fulfill my assignment by skimming the manuscript and thinking of a few nice things to say about the book and author. The fact is, however, that the book grabbed my attention and I couldn't stop reading it, underlining, and writing notes in the margin. This is a very good book. I wish I had read it years ago as I made fumbling and now embarrassing attempts to be a "prophetic preacher." I was so sure of myself: so sure that by scolding my congregation—all of whose members were as old as my parents and grandparents—they would see the righteousness of my words and become less racist, less sexist, less classist, and so on. I wish I had had the opportunity to hear a wise scholar/pastor point out, as Walter does here, that the great prophets of Israel only rarely addressed specific social issues and generally were not advocates for particular causes, as is the case with much liberal prophetic preaching today. They could, on occasion, be stunningly specific: one thinks of rigged scales in the market place. But more often, Walter explains, the prophets "aim beyond and beneath specific issues to the underlying governance of YHWH and the profound way in which Jerusalem must come to terms with that governance" (p. 60). I could have used that information when, in the first year of my ordained ministry, I charged into a controversial social and political issue—in that instance, whether the town should build a system to bring lake water to the community rather than relying on the iron-laced water from the town well—and took a side, in the process irritating quite a few members of the congregation and the community and losing a few members whom the congregation could not afford to lose—all over lake water. I thought I was being a prophetic minister.

I wish I had read Walter Brueggemann explain that "the prophetic is not, contrary to some conservative views, a matter of prediction. Nor is it, contrary to some liberal views, a nagging or a scolding or righteous indignation about social justice" (p. 132).

Looking back now, when the congregation and I got it right—as when we opened our new building for a day school for the children of migrant workers who came to northwest Indiana to work in the fields during the summer—it was not because I had scolded them but because they heard a biblical mandate to love neighbors and to stand with the poor. In Walter's image, the people allowed the preacher to help them root themselves, "embed" themselves in the text and in the prophetic tradition. They did something that would have been unimaginable before—they opened their new building to the children of strangers.

If it is not nagging, scolding, or self-righteous pontificating, what exactly *is* prophetic preaching? Brueggemann says, and uses this as the fundamental theme of the book, that prophetic preaching is "a sustained effort to imagine the world as though YHWH were a real character and the defining agent in the life of the world" (p. 132).

True prophetic preaching is witness, affirmation, proclamation that God is, that God reigns, and that God does not abandon or forget. It is, simply, publicly articulated belief in God. The current climate for this public articulation is ambiguous at best. On the one hand, there are the purveyors of the prosperity gospel who claim, apparently without much concentrated time reading the Bible, that God will bless those who believe fervently enough with this world's goods, wealth, health, and success. On the other hand are the neo-atheists who sell a lot of books claiming that the whole religion project is anti-scientific, unreasonable nonsense, if it is not positively lethal. There is no God, they insist, and the sooner we acknowledge that, the better off we will be. And multitudes of others—even if they do not go so far as to buy the neo-atheists' books or gather under their banner—are nevertheless their acolytes when they simply act as if there were no god; they are implicit atheists. In the prevalent American predilection for an "irrelevant transcendence" and a "cozy immanence" Brueggemann perceives the pet gods of our culture.

Walter Brueggemann has taught us, over the years, to be careful not to circumscribe God. He has reminded us that God cannot be contained in human thought and rhetoric, even theological thought and rhetoric. He instructed us to be modest when speaking about God. He models the lesson himself by declining to translate into English the Hebrew construct *YHWH*, which designates the Holy One, the "I Am Who I Will Be" of Israel. Walter's honest, eloquent, and powerful prayers in *Awed to Heaven, Rooted in Earth* reflect that appropriate theological humility by not using other prayerful modes of address that are so commonly and thoughtlessly used.

The prophetic tradition, on the other hand, proclaims a God who is an active agent, who is manifestly present in the life of the world and is always up to the business of creating newness. "I am about to do a new thing; do you not perceive it?" (Isa. 43:19). It is precisely when we take the world seriously that the prophetic tradition becomes critical and complex—and urgent. Not unlike former St. Louis Cardinal pitcher Bob Gibson's fastball, says Brueggemann, a devout and long-standing partisan of the Cardinals. "Of such pitches, the commentators say that they 'pop,' they 'move,' they 'surge,' they surprise, they overwhelm" (p. 25).

The future preacher will live in a world different from our own, in a culture rapidly changing in front of our eyes, and for those of us who are at home in the United States, in a nation that has sustained very significant loss. At the moment the U.S. economy is in shambles, a credit crisis narrowly averted but not addressed. The future will be one in which the United States will not likely be the sole economic super power and the model to which the rest of the world aspires. Brueggemann underscores several times the reality that continues to shock Americans, that a strong military cannot always have its way in the world and that our refusal to invest in education almost guarantees that our favorite narratives of technological self-sufficiency will not long hold. We live, Brueggemann says, in an "ocean of anxiety" (p. 18).

The most significant change looming over everything else is what happened on September 11, 2001. On that day, Brueggemann points out, we Americans lost more than buildings and almost three thousand lives, tragic as that was. We also lost our sense of invulnerability. And nothing our government has done since, including two wars and an intensive, tedious, and invasive security system at our airports, has made us feel safe.

Those are new realities for the next generation of preachers to confront. Brueggemann uses the categories of denial and despair to describe it. Nostalgia for the world we lost is palpable: the ritual singing of "God Bless America" is, Brueggemann says, a plea to give us back the world we have lost.

Far better and more helpful is to read Scripture. The Bible knows a lot about loss, lament, and grief. Brueggemann's treatment of the eighth-century prophets—that extraordinary sequence of Amos, Hosea, Micah, and Isaiah of Jerusalem, who called Israel back to covenantal faithfulness—and the sixth-century prophets of Second Isaiah and Jeremiah, and the Psalm writers, who deal with the crushing loss of Jerusalem, is the most helpful thing I have ever read about these topics.

Many in Israel could not imagine a world without Jerusalem, the Temple, or the Davidic monarchy. The events of destruction, exile, and discontinuity were more devastating than anyone could imagine. Prophets deal with loss, prophetic narrative hovers over our loss and grief. And here Brueggemann becomes pastorally helpful to the reader.

Our culture is inclined to hurry past loss and grief, to rush too quickly to resolution. "Everything will be all right," we assure ourselves, when everything is not at all right. The best and most sensitive of us know this in our preaching and pastoral care. But no one is immune to the deep inclination to "get over it" and move on. The prophets know about loss and grief, and Brueggemann supplies a wealth of textural material to illustrate.

As I write this, I am also planning a memorial service, something we pastors regularly do. A bright, lively, articulate, funny young woman, thirty-seven years old, has died. She was an officer in the congregation with many friends. Two years ago she was diagnosed with brain cancer. Her journey was not untypical: radiation, chemotherapy, remission, then more radiation and chemotherapy, a gradual weakening as the disease spread; and we, her minister and friends, watched and prayed for and with her. She died this week; and it would not honor her or her friends to hurry past her dying too quickly. The Bible, the prophets, know about loss and the importance of dwelling with it.

Walter Brueggemann reminds that there is always also a movement toward hope. It is not an add-on: hope is not a belated afterthought. Hope is "intrinsic to the prophetic message" (p. 111). The great prophetic themes of destruction and restoration are reenacted in the central Christian themes of crucifixion and resurrection. God, the prophets imagine, is always doing a new thing, creating a way where there is no way, bringing life out of death, light out of very real darkness.

At the memorial service for my young friend, I will read gratefully the words of the prophet:

> The LORD is the everlasting God,
> . . . .
> He does not faint or grow weary;
> . . . .
> those who wait for the LORD shall renew their strength,
>   they shall mount up with wings like eagles,
> they shall run and not be weary,
>   they shall walk and not faint. (Isa. 40:28b, 30, 31)

The practice of prophetic imagination is, this good book reminds us, a decision to believe and trust that God reigns. It is to imagine the world as God intends it and as God works to bring it about. It is never to deny or hurry past loss and grief. It is to remember—always—that "weeping may linger for the night, but joy comes with the morning" (Ps. 30:5b).

John M. Buchanan
Pastor, Fourth Presbyterian Church
Chicago, Ill.

CHAPTER 1

The Narrative Embedment
of Prophetic Preaching

IT IS MY HOPE, in what follows, to make a credible connection between the material of "prophetic utterance" in the Old Testament itself and the actual practice of "prophetic preaching" that is mandated in the actual work of pastors who are located in worshipping congregations. It is not difficult to see what the prophets of the Old Testament are doing, and we have ample interpretive analyses of that work.[1] But the transposition from that ancient clarity to contemporary social, ecclesial reality is not easy or obvious.[2] "Prophetic preaching," undertaken by working pastors, is profoundly difficult and leaves the preacher in an ambiguous and exposed position. The task is difficult because such a preacher must at the same time "speak truth" while maintaining a budget, a membership, and a program in a context that is often not prepared for such truthfulness. Indeed, given the seductions and accommodations of many congregations, not to mention larger judicatories in the church, such venues are often not readily venues for truth-telling.

Given that problematic reality that is ubiquitous and systemic, we may also note that "prophetic preaching" is not in its definition obvious. On the one hand and popularly, "prophetic preaching" may mean to take up the great issues of the day, so that the preacher is cast, with some immediacy, in the role of prophet. On the other hand, it is possible to construe "prophetic preaching" as a probe of ancient prophetic texts with inescapable side glances at contemporary issues. This latter perspective focuses on texts rather than immediate contemporary context; in many congregations this is a more viable approach

1

that may lead, on occasion, to direct or implied connections. My own judgment is that for most preachers in most congregational settings, a focus on the biblical prophetic text—with traces that connect to contemporaneity—is a more realistic way to proceed. For that reason I have elsewhere suggested that the preacher may be a "scribe" who handles old texts and permits them to be seen with contemporary force and authority.[3] In such an approach, the preacher-scribe is not cast as a prophet but as a handler of the prophetic tradition who brings to availability a treasure of what is old (tradition) and what is new (contemporaneity) (Matt. 13:51-53). It will be this latter perspective that I pursue in this discussion.

I

When I ponder what the ancient prophets in Israel are doing as we have them in the text, I arrive at this judgment that will serve as my guiding thesis: prophetic proclamation is an attempt to imagine the world as though YHWH—the creator of the world, the deliverer of Israel, the Father of our Lord Jesus Christ whom we Christians come to name as Father, Son, and Spirit—were a real character and an effective agent in the world. I use the subjunctive "were" because such a claim is not self-evident and remains to be established again and again in every such utterance. The key term in my thesis is "imagine," that is, to utter, entertain, describe, and construe a world other than the one that is manifest in front to us, for that present world is readily and commonly taken without such agency or character for YHWH. Thus the offer of prophetic imagination is one that contradicts the taken-for-granted world around us.[4]

At the outset, it is clear that this way of putting the matter refuses two common assumptions. On the one hand, it rejects the more conservative assumption that the prophets were predictors, those who tell the future, with particular reference to predictions of the coming Christ. On the other hand, this thesis refuses the common liberal assumption that the prophets were social activists who worked to establish social justice. It strikes me that the ancient prophets only rarely took up any concrete social issue. More important to them than concrete social issues is the fact that they characteristically spoke in poetic idiom with rich metaphors, so that their language is recurringly teasing, elusive, and evocative, with lesser accent on instruction or didacticism.[5]

My thesis about "imagining" with reference to YHWH exposes two common seductions about our characteristic theological speech. It is not easy or obvious about how to "imagine YHWH" because the God of Israel fits none of our conventional theological categories. On the one hand, we tend to imagine the world with reference to other gods, that is, by a practice of *idolatry*. Thus we imagine the world according to a remote God who is not involved in the world and who could not intervene in the world; thus "rational Christians" may regard "an interventionist God" as a silly notion. Or we take God as a pet who is preoccupied with our well-being, or variously as the god of nation, party, race, gender, or ideology. Thus the temptation is to an *irrelevant transcendence* or a *cozy immanence*. None of these conventional ways serves well the hard, dangerous work of "imagining YHWH."

On the other hand, perhaps more likely, we imagine the world with reference to no god at all, that is, as *atheism*.[6] We reduce reality to manageable proportion, imagine our autonomy with accountability to no one, a matter of "might makes right" or simply that it is all "a tale told by an idiot signifying nothing." While such atheism is a persistent possibility in modern rationality, it is most often the case that some idol lurks at the edge of such atheism, so that idolatry is surely the more immediate and compelling temptation.[7] The prophetic task of "imagining YHWH" flies in the face of our *conventional idolatries* and/or our *conventional atheisms*. The task requires courage and unfettered imagination as well as categories that are unsettling and subversive of the way we conventionally prefer to construe reality.

Given my thesis that imagining YHWH as a real character and as an effective agent in the world leads then to a second, derivative thesis: prophetic proclamation is the staging and performance of a contest between two narrative accounts of the world and an effort to show that the YHWH account of reality is more adequate and finally more reliable than the dominant narrative account that is cast among us as though it were true and beyond critique.[8] This performed contestation between narratives is modeled in narrative simplicity and directness in Elijah's contest at Mt. Carmel in which he defiantly requires a decision between narratives and so between gods: "How long will you go limping with two different opinions? If the LORD is God, follow him; but if Baal, then follow him" (1 Kgs. 18:21). This dramatic utterance is in fact a summary of a long, vigorous contestation between two narratives and two consequent construals of reality.[9]

The present form of that contestation, I propose, is the felt and often denied tension between the gospel narrative that specializes in social transformation, justice, and compassion and the dominant narrative of our culture that I have elsewhere termed "military consumerism."[10] The contestation that is constituted by prophetic preaching is in our own time, as always, profoundly difficult because the dominant narrative, the one contradicted by the narrative of YHWH, is seldom recognized as a social construction and is almost never lined out in its full clarity and claim. The contestation, moreover, is difficult because the YHWH narrative is rarely recognized as a genuine alternative to the dominant narrative and is more often reckoned as a footnote or a pin prick to the dominant narrative but not a real alternative. In our time and circumstance, the narrative of US military consumerism and the YHWH narrative of social transformation, justice, and compassion are deeply intertwined and there is great resistance to sorting them out.[11]

Thus I suggest that prophetic preaching can take place only where the preacher is deeply embedded in the YHWH narrative. When the listening community is also embedded there or at least has a residual attachment to that narrative, a chance for engagement is offered. In most ecclesial practice, the sign of congregational embedment or residual attachment to that YHWH narrative is baptism that gives dramatic access to that alternative narrative. Membership in that alternative narrative is consequently realized and enhanced through socialization in education and pastoral nurture. Thus prophetic preaching takes place in a context where a very different subversive conversation about reality is available. In many church contexts, of course, the possibility for such a conversation is eroded or compromised. Such erosion or compromise makes the task more difficult but for that reason also more urgent.

II

The backdrop of prophetic preaching is the dispute between narratives. Many congregations and many preachers would much prefer to keep that dispute hidden or silenced. But the dispute is characteristically present in any case, as the adherents to the dominant narrative are acutely vigilant about any hint that that narrative may be placed in question.

The dominant narrative—one I have characterized as "therapeutic, technological, consumerist militarism"—is committed to the notion of *self-invention* in the pursuit of *self-sufficiency*. Between a beginning in self-invention and a culmination in self-sufficiency, that narrative enjoins to *competitive productivity*, motivated by pervasive anxiety about having enough, or being enough, or being in control. Thus it is an acting out, in quotidian ways, of the modern sense of an autonomous self that eventuates in a rat race that readily culminates in violence if and when that self is impinged upon in inconvenient ways. That dominant narrative is seldom lined out, rarely seen in its coherence, and hardly ever critiqued in its elemental claims. That, I propose, is the matrix for prophetic preaching. In ancient Israel it was a matrix governed by the unconditional claim of the Davidic dynasty and the perpetual guarantee of divine presence in the Jerusalem temple, both claims exploited by King Solomon in his propensity to accumulation. In the contemporary United States, it is a matrix that in parallel fashion is rooted in a conviction concerning *US exceptionalism* that gives warrant to the usurpatious pursuit of commodities in the name of freedom, at the expense of the neighbor.[12]

Prophetic preaching is rooted in the alternative narrative of the God of Israel. Like the dominant narrative, that alternative narrative can also be lined out in various modes:

1. In the Old Testament, that alternative narrative is given succinct expression in what Gerhard von Rad termed Israel's "credo," which features the promise to the ancestors, the Exodus deliverance, and the entry into the land of promise, all accomplished by the powerful fidelity of YHWH.[13] At core, Israel confessed: "The LORD brought us out of Egypt with a mighty hand and an outstretched arm, with a terrifying display of power, and with signs and wonders; and he brought us into this place and gave us this land, a land flowing with milk and honey" (Deut. 26:8-9). One need not follow von Rad's now doubted critical judgments to see this recital as a reliable summary of core faith in Israel.

2. In the New Testament, the counterpoint to von Rad's "credo" is given, as C. H. Dodd averred, in the Pauline summary witness of 1 Corinthians 15:3-5:[14] "For I handed on to you as of first importance what I in turn had received: that Christ died for our sins in accordance with the scriptures, and that he was buried, and that he was raised on the third day in accordance with the scriptures . . ." Of this statement, Dodd judges, "The Pauline *kerygma*, therefore, is a proclamation of the facts of death and resurrection of Christ in an eschatological setting which gives significance to the facts."[15] Here the narrative revolves around Christ, but clearly it assumes the action of the God of Israel who is the God of the church.

3. In the normative narrative of the church, the same story is recited in the classic formulations of the Nicene Creed and the Apostles Creed, both of which pivot on the incarnation, on the death and resurrection of Christ.

4. In a classic Jewish statement, Franz Rosenzweig has lined out the faith of Judaism under the rubrics of "Creation-Revelation-Redemption."[16]

These several tellings of "the old, old story" of course yield different accents. They are, however, agreed that YHWH (in Christian confession, the Father of our Lord Jesus Christ) is the deciding character and key agent in the historical-cosmic process. While the variations are of course significant, the commonality of all of these tellings is evident when it is contrasted with the dominant narrative of *self-invention*, *competitive productivity*, and *self-sufficiency*, a narrative without the defining agency of YHWH.

One could make the argument that I seek to make here about prophetic preaching by appeal to any of these versions of the narrative. Here I will pursue my theme of the narrative embedment of prophetic preaching with reference to the Pentateuch, which is, as von Rad has shown, the core narrative of Israel writ large. It is clear that that narrative in the Old Testament, in its many variations, is offered as an alternative, a contradiction, and a subversion of the dominant narrative that was all around Israel, variously as "Canaanite religion" (in the case of Elijah) or the imperial imposition of a series of superpowers. *Mutatis mutandis*, the apostolic witness of the New Testament was an alternative to various narrative offers, notably that of Roman power legitimated by Roman religion.[17]

Thus the prophetic preacher is grounded in that alternative narrative that insists upon discerning life with reference to the God who dominates and occupies that narrative. The preacher thus has at hand the materials out of which to continue to "imagine" YHWH. In moving from such narrative embedment:

- The preacher must keep deciding in pastoral ways about the means and pace for advocating this narrative in such a contested environment wherein many listeners have no zeal about such contestation and do not want the dominant narrative placed in question.
- The preacher must be continually aware of the many and deep ways in which the dominant narrative is defining for her own life, so that no one of us is immune to the contradiction that is to be faced.
- The preacher must remember that when the congregation (or some part of it) is deeply and convincedly embedded in the dominant narrative, prophetic preaching that advocates the counter-narrative sounds like unbearable nonsense. I believe that such an "epistemological misfit" is defining for prophetic preaching, as it must have been in ancient Israel. From the perspective of the dominant narrative, advocacy of this alternative narrative sounds at best like foolishness, thus the foolishness of such preaching (1 Cor. 1:18-25).

III

Thus I consider the pentateuchal narrative as the base and assumption for prophetic preaching in the Old Testament. That no doubt is how the canon of the Old Testament is arranged, an arrangement that subsequently came to be tagged as "the law and the prophets," that is, the Torah corpus of the

Pentateuch and the prophetic corpus that follows. Such a canonical arrangement, it will be recognized, is in tension with what has become the accepted critical judgment that the prophetic corpus in fact is antecedent to the formation of the Pentateuch in the sixth-fifth centuries BCE.[18] While acknowledging the force of that critical judgment, it is not unreasonable to proceed here on the basis of the canonical arrangement, recognizing that I am engaged in a post-critical interpretation that is not uninformed by critical perspective.[19]

1. At the center of the pentateuchal narrative is the core presentation of Moses. He is the dominant figure in the narrative, and for that reason it is not surprising that he has traditionally been taken as the author of the narrative. The "Mosaic center" features three narrative themes:[20]

(a) The Exodus deliverance is a divine emancipation of slaves wrought through a daring human agent. The narrative account of Exodus 1–15 moves from *the cry of distress* on the lips of the slaves (Exod. 2:23-24) to *the celebrative elation* of the emancipated slaves (Exod. 15:1-18, 20-21). That movement from cry to joy is defining for the narrative; conversely the well-being of the empire, the great adversary of YHWH, is reduced to a desperate cry (Exod. 12:29-32).[21] There is no doubt that the same movement from cry to joy is reflected in the terse teaching of Jesus: "Blessed are you who weep now, for you will laugh. . . . Woe to you who are laughing now, for you will mourn and weep" (Luke 6:21, 25). It is clear that the exodus is accomplished by the will, power, and transformative energy of YHWH, an affirmation voiced in the singing of Israel:

> He sent darkness, and made the land dark;
> . . . .
> He struck down all the firstborn in their land,
>   the first issue of all their strength. . . .
> . . . .
> Egypt was glad when they departed,
>   for dread of them had fallen upon it. (Ps. 105:28, 36, 38)

It is clear, at the same time, that the exodus depended upon willing human agency, for it is Moses who is dispatched to Pharaoh: "So come, I will send you to Pharaoh to bring my people, the Israelites, out of Egypt" (Exod. 3:10; see Ps. 105:26-27). The narrative easily asserts "double agency" about the act of emancipation, an assertion that pervades Israel's memory.

(b) The tradition of wilderness sojourn is "travel music" from bondage to new land. The music performs the arid, destitute travel of faith in territory that lacks a viable life support system. The narrative tells of the desperate anxiety and protest of emancipated Israel and the responsive action of YHWH in providing meat, bread, and water in a context where there was none. It turns out, in Israel's telling, that the power of YHWH transformed a milieu of death into one of fruitful sustenance. It is that transformative capacity of which Israel continues to sing:

> The wilderness and dry land shall be glad,
>   the desert shall rejoice and blossom;
> like the crocus it shall blossom abundantly,
>   and rejoice with joy and singing. (Isaiah 35:1)

> I will open rivers on the bare heights,
>   and fountains in the midst of the valleys;
> I will make the wilderness a pool of water,
>   and the dry land spring of water.
> I will put in the wilderness the cedar,
>   the acacia, the myrtle, and the olive;
> I will set in the desert the cypress,
>   the plane and the pine together,
> so that all may see and know,
>   all may consider and understand,
> that the hand of the LORD has done this,
>   the Holy One of Israel has created it. (Isa. 41:18-20)

(c) At Sinai, Israel gladly received Torah commandments as an alternative to the coercive commands of Pharaoh (Exod. 19:8). Israel received the Decalogue (Exod. 20:21-17) and swore allegiance to the God of covenant who is the God of emancipation (Exod. 24:3, 7). The outcome is that Israel is shaped as a community of listening obedience whose life is from YHWH, the God of emancipation, whose life is to be lived back to YHWH in grateful response.

This sequence of a) *cry to joy*, b) *faithful transformative sustenance*, and c) *listening obedience* becomes the defining accent for the life of Israel that is lived in dialogic engagement with YHWH. It is this dialogic engagement that constitutes Israel's life as a people holy to YHWH (Exod. 19:5-6).

2. The "canonical" narrative of exodus-wilderness, sojourn-Sinai covenant takes on a continuing life in the traditioning processes of Israel, a process that has been awkwardly but powerfully articulated in the "Documentary Hypothesis" of nineteenth-century scholarship.[22] The ongoing interpretive

process (that yielded the materials of Exodus, Leviticus, Numbers, and Deuteronomy) exhibits the way in which the covenant of Sinai is subsequently codified to remain contemporary in Israel, always for a new time, a new place, and a new circumstance.

On the one hand, that codification led to the so-called "Priestly" materials of Exodus-Leviticus-Numbers, a careful articulation of holy times, holy places, and holy people that could give Israel a quite distinct identity as the people of YHWH amid the peoples of the world. On the other hand, more pertinent and more interesting for our topic, the Sinai tradition was alternatively codified in the tradition of Deuteronomy. That tradition has a remarkably supple dynamism that permitted the Torah of Sinai to be always again reformulated in fresh terms.[23] Thus the Torah requirements of the book of Deuteronomy move from the Sinai formulation in contemporizing ways. The covenant is eventually given articulation as an unaccommodating quid-pro-quo structure of obedience-blessing or alternatively, disobedience-curse:

> See, I have set before you today life and prosperity, death and adversity. If you obey the commandments of the LORD your God that I am commanding you today, by loving the LORD your God, walking in his ways, and observing his commandments, decrees, and ordinances, then you shall live and become numerous, and the LORD your God will bless you in the land that you are entering to possess. But if your heart turns away and you do not hear, but are led astray to bow down to other gods and serve them, I declare to you today that you shall perish; you shall not live long in the land that you are crossing the Jordan to enter and possess. . . . Choose life so that you and your descendants may live . . . (Deut. 30:15-10)

Israel's continued life in the abundant land of promise is made closely conditioned on the basis of Torah-keeping. Through the interpretive process, *the gifts of YHWH* (blessings of creation, miracles of history) and *YHWH's claims* on Israel's life through Torah commandments are made defining and non-negotiable for the public life of Israel and, by derivation, for the public life of the world.

This succinct formulation of quid pro quo is decisive for what follows in prophetic preaching, even as it is exceedingly difficult in the modern world. It is plausible, of course, to take that characteristic covenantal formulation in a flat "supernatural" sense that makes it easy to dismiss in the modern world. It is also possible, however, to see the quid-pro-quo formulation of Deuteronomy as a shrewd discernment of the governance of the world that cannot be mocked, a givenness that is, in Israel's parlance, guaranteed by the creator God. Thus the *Sinai formulation* is linked to the *givenness of the created order*. The God of covenant is the creator God. This connection, especially articulated by Hans Heinrich Schmid, permits the judgment that Deuteronomy is informed by the observant shrewdness of the wisdom teachers who eschew a crude supernaturalism but who nonetheless see that ethical requirements and limits of lived reality are acknowledged so that actions bring with them inescapable consequences.[24] The world, in this purview, is morally coherent and is guaranteed by the God who occupies the narrative of Exodus-sojourn-Sinai. It is impossible to understand the movement of the Old Testament from the Torah to the prophets unless this defining conviction about YHWH's governance is fully recognized. At the same time, it is important to recognize how such a discernment of reality, given with narrative particularity, flies in the face of modernist notions of autonomy.

3. The Mosaic narrative in the Pentateuch has as its introduction two narrative accounts of unexpected gifts from YHWH that are completely inexplicable:

(a) The creation narrative of Genesis 1, also likely an exilic act of defiant hope, witnesses to the way in which God, by an issue of command, "calls the world into being."[25] The vision of Genesis 1 concerns an inexplicable miracle from God that has as its outcome a teeming abundance of fruitfulness in the earth. The narrative of God's initiatory goodness is antecedent to any notion of parsimony, because YHWH's will for life provides for all of creation.

(b) The wonder of creation is matched in the ancestral narratives of Genesis 12–50 with the capacity of God to call forth, in each successive generation, a faithful people that has itself reached a dead end. The narrative is shot through with the promissory resolve of YHWH. Writ large, the promises of YHWH concern a land for the family of Abraham and Sarah that is also to be blessing to the families of the nations (Gen. 12:3). But those large promises depend upon the intimate promise made to the old couple, Abraham and Sarah. In their aging days, Abraham, "as good as dead" (Heb. 11:12), and Sarah received a promise from God: "I will surely return to you in due season, and your wife Sarah shall have a son" (Gen. 18:10). By the end of the narrative, it is affirmed that God can do the impossible: "Is anything too wonderful for the LORD?" (Gen. 18:14). The rhetorical question receives a "no" in the tradition: no, it is not impossible for God! It is impossible for the old couple to have a son and an heir. The entire narrative of Genesis turns on this divine impossibility, a wonder that is reenacted in subsequent generations for a series of barren women.[26] The entire future of Israel depends, in each generation, on the capacity and resolve of YHWH to make a way out of no way. This reiterated miracle of new life in a context of hopelessness evokes in Israel a due sense of awe that issues in doxology. Well, it issues in laughter: "Now Sarah said, 'God has brought laughter for me; everyone who hears will laugh with me'" (Gen. 21:6). In subsequent Christian tradition, that laugh has become an "Easter laugh," a deep sweep of elation that looks death and despair in the face and mocks them. The ancestral narratives attest to the power of YHWH to create new historical possibilities where there is no ground for expectation.

IV

This complex, thick, multilayered narrative provides the theological accents and the interpretive nerve that permit Israel to contest the dominant narrative of the world that is told and retold all around Israel by those who want to talk Israel out of its distinctive narrative and its dangerous, undomesticated imagination. That narrative (and its ongoing imaginative force), however, continue to sustain faithful Israel and make Israel an inconvenience in the world of the dominant narrative. Before we move on to prophetic preaching, we may consider, in three perspectives, the insistent, generative force of this counter narrative:

1. The Pentateuchal narrative posits and permits a series of convictions that could be attested in a variety of ways:

- The world begins in wonder concerning the inexplicable abundance willed by God the creator.
- The history and future of this peculiar people depends upon the inexplicable gift of an heir, so that the force of familial blessing is given, generation by generation, albeit always at the last minute.
- The work of Moses, at the behest of YHWH, is the emancipation of the slaves from Pharaoh's cheap labor program. The God of the exodus exhibits a solidarity with the exploited slaves of the empire and an alert edge about undoing that exploitation that is enacted by political imagination and courage.
- The work of Moses is to manage the process of inexplicable nurture and nourishment in an environment where no such resources were on offer. It is the astonished awareness of Israel that the gifts of life are wondrously given in contexts of chaos and death.

- The work of Moses is to administer the process whereby a covenant is enacted between holy God and historical people, a covenant that assured that the emancipated people will continue to live its life in emancipatory ways that defy all conventional notions of injustice.[27]
- The ongoing tradition of Deuteronomy, subsequent to Moses, exhibits the interpretive elasticity of the Mosaic memory and transposes the covenant of Sinai into a theology of accountability in which Israel's future depends upon adherence to non-negotiable Torah.
- The destiny of Moses and Israel is to wait. That wait is marked by confidence in God's fidelity; but it is by faith and not by sight. Moses can see the land of promise, but he cannot see how it will be given or received.

The large sweep of this normative narrative moves from initial wonder (Genesis, twice) to expectant waiting (Deut. 34). In that move *from wonder to wait* by way of covenant, YHWH is placed front and center in the life of Israel and, derivatively, in the life of the world. The story of Israel cannot be told or received without the central character, who defies all political and epistemological conventions.

2. On all counts, this narrative, with its move from wonder to wait, contradicts the narrative of self-invention, competitive productivity, and self-sufficiency. Israel's life is a life that contradicts the way of the world:

- Wonder instead of self-invention;
- Emancipation instead of the rat race of production;
- Nourishment instead of labor for that which does not satisfy;
- Covenantal dialogue instead of tyrannical monopoly or autonomous anxiety;
- A quid pro quo of accountability instead of either abdicating submissiveness or autonomous self-assertion;
- Waiting instead of having or despair about not having.

At every accent point in the narrative, the tradition of Israel asserts that the dominant narrative of the world is not adequate and so cannot be true. It cannot be adequate because it omits the defining resolve and capacity of YHWH, the lead character in the life of the world.

3. In the New Testament and the Christian tradition, the ancient story of Israel is retold with reference to Jesus. This is not to say it is a better rendering that supersedes that of Israel; of course not. It is only to recognize that it is a

different rendering, but one that cannot be understood without reference to the more ancient rendering. In Christian tradition,

- The wonder of creation is cast as the wonder of Christ's birth, surrounded by angels and guiding star;
- The requirements of covenant are exhibited in the public ministry of Jesus and in his summons to discipleship. As Israel is called at Sinai to a distinct identity, so Christ's call to discipleship is a summons to join his alternative practice of reality. Because his summons contests the dominant regime (the empire of Rome), he was executed (crucifixion) by the empire through which the dominant narrative has its Friday moment of prevailing.
- His resurrection (and ultimate return in power) is an act of waiting on the part of the church for gifts that are yet to be given and promises that are yet to be kept.

I have no wish to force Israel's narrative into the categories of Christian formulation or to insist on exact counterpoints between the traditions. My intent is only to suggest that the ancient narrative of Israel—retold in Judaism— and the Christian rendering of the same narrative share, in the face of the dominant narrative, a peculiar narrative made peculiar by the character who occupies center stage.[28] It is, of course, impossible to tell this story without the defining agency of YHWH who is decisive in every point of the story. It is for that reason that every critical attempt to discern or "explain" the story on historical grounds is bound to be inadequate and to fail. There is no story without the character of YHWH. At the same time, we must recognize that the telling of this story is an enormous act of imagination. It is on the lips of the storytellers that YHWH takes on life. It is always easy enough for adherents of the dominant story to dismiss this alternative narrative because YHWH, the defining agent in that narrative, does not even register in the categories of the dominant narrative.

Thus it is the work of endless reperformance to continue to make this alternative account of reality available and persuasive. It is for that reason that the narrative itself, in Exodus 12–13, takes such care to instruct about the proper reperformance of the narrative at Passover. It is for the same reason, moreover, that Paul twice underscores the traditioning process alive, once with reference to the crucifixion-resurrection and once with reference to the Eucharist as the matrix for the narrative (1 Cor. 11:23-26; 15:3-8). Prophetic preaching depends upon the regular reperformance of this narrative that presents YHWH, the agent of wonder and nourishment, the giver of commandments who presides over our waiting, as the defining reality of the world. It is this retelling that creates an environment for prophetic preaching. And where the narrative is not kept available and persuasive in all its scandalous force, prophetic preaching has little chance of being either uttered or heard.

V

Israel's narrative account of reality has been a matter of contestation with other narrative accounts of reality since its earliest formulation—whenever that was. As we have it, the initial contestation is between Pharaoh (bricks without straw) and YHWH ("Let my people go") (Exod. 5:1-9). The plague narratives in Exodus 6–11 constitute a script for dramatic performance of the contest between two narrative accounts of reality, a contest that reaches its denouement in Exodus 8:18 wherein the Egyptians reach their limit—except that the contest persists even after that dramatic limit.[29] The contest in the book of Exodus (and thereafter), moreover, is not on level ground. In that narrative and everywhere, the dominant narrative (in this case the narrative of Pharaoh) has the upper hand, enjoying public legitimacy, liturgical reinforcement, and technological superiority. Thus Israel's narrative is characteristically told "from below," at a disadvantage, mostly by the socially disadvantaged, so that it appears to be "weak and foolish" in the eyes of the world. It is in the nature of the case that Israel, even among its own, must struggle to make the case for the legitimacy and adequacy of its narrative account of the world.

And we, as belated practitioners of that narrative, participate in the same contestation with the same disadvantages, through the same struggle, even when the struggle is a "clash within."[30] Thus we are always being asked, and we ourselves are always asking:

- Is this account of reality historically reliable—did it really happen? The question of course reflects skepticism that is sponsored by a modern historicist rationality. It is a question not asked by serious practitioners or liturgical performers of the narrative. Except of course, we ourselves are double-minded. We ourselves know about historical criticism, about the drift of contemporary scholarship toward a dismissal of any ground for the historicity of this narrative in any of is crucial parts.[31]
- Is it morally acceptable? We ourselves cringe from the violence enacted in the narrative, violence that is either perpetrated by or

authorized by YHWH. We wonder how the God of the narrative could bear the drowning death of the Egyptians or the savage slaughter of the Canaanites.[32]

- Is it imaginatively evocative enough for the profound emotional extremities wherein our humanness is adjudicated? The narrative is not much given to empathetic emotional extremes that we face in contemporary life, and we have to ask if ancient offers of agony and ecstasy, of hurt and elation, are adequate for the life we live. Does this cry and this dance ring true among us?

- Can this narrative make us happy? We ask amid the narrative of consumerism that makes a promise about ease, comfort, and convenience that the old narratives do not have in purview.

- Can this narrative make us safe? How could we trust in miracles in the face of real raw power in the world?

The narrative is problematic enough that we can give no easy answers to these serious questions. But we must answer as best we can. The answers we give, I suspect, are most often grounded in a resolve and a certainty that provides answers, but our resolve and certitude do not arise from those sorts of answers. Rather it is the other way round. We have, in ways we do not understand, arrived a priori about loyalty to this narrative account of the world, and in some great measure the answers we give to these questions are in fact irrelevant to our own commitment. And when we answer in what we wish were persuasive ways, we really want our conversation partners to accept in trust what we accept in trust. These are "reasons of the heart" that do not yield syllogistic certainty. The certitude and resolve for us is a gift not thought but known more deeply.

But of course we give the best answers we can muster:

- Is it historically reliable? We refuse modern historicist questions and readily make a distinction between positivistic history and the generative power of memory.[33] We know very well that the text to some great extent has arisen from a later traditioning process and is a social construction. We are quick to point out, however, that the dominant narrative account of military consumerism is a social construction wrought by loud ideologues. And so as fully as care about reliability, we finally assert that whatever may be the "data," we stake our lives on it, and live, as best we are able, in the world mandated by this narrative.

- Is it morally acceptable? We have found a variety of ways to cope with the moral repugnance of the violence perpetrated and authorized by God. We rely, generally, on an evolutionary hypothesis that locates such violence in primitive projection and in any case, we say it is human projection. My own response to the question wants to refuse easy answers about evolution and projection to say that the God given here is in the process, obvious in the text, of recovery from real violence.[34] And in any case, we say, other competing narratives are more readily committed to violence, notably the narrative of the national security state with its apparent commitment to perpetual war.[35]

- Can it make us happy? We are able to cite wondrous cases of those who have lived and died in this narrative and have found joy, because the God of this narrative is our heart's true desire. We slightly change the subject, because the outcome is not the happiness conjured by consumer ads; it is the joy that comes of being in sync with one's true character, to come down where we ought to be. We note, moreover, that the dominant narrative does not yield happiness, if the indices of social misery are a measure of what that narrative yields.[36]

- Can this narrative make us safe? The practitioners of this narrative are not kept safe by the measure of the world. They are safe only when we fall back into God's providential assurance that the hairs of our heads will be counted and our names will be written in the book of life.[37] But then, we say that the dominant narrative is a powerful generator of anxiety and "Security," as in "Homeland" is a mockery and a farce, for such a narrative yields no safety, and we refuse to live perpetually on Orange Alert.

VI

The prophetic preacher, as a child of this narrative, lives in some dis-ease. Because such a child of the narrative is not naïve about the challenges and the risks of the narrative. Such a preacher may entertain all kinds of doubts and misgivings but is capable of a willing, obedient suspension of disbelief. Such hard-won innocence does not pretend or cover up but appeals to a deeper claim that defies the skepticism of modernist rationality:

- Such a preacher knows about social construction of the narrative but does not doubt that there is more here than ideological construction.

- Such a preacher cringes at the violence and moral repugnance in the narrative but knows that at bottom the social process is conflicted and problematic at best.
- Such a preacher has learned to live with the imaginative force of the narrative and finds the self led, perhaps by the Spirit, to see connections been the ancient text and contemporary lived reality. That preacher is aware of the thin artistry of contemporary sitcoms and professional sports and what passes for political discourse and knows that, by contrast, the artistry to the narrative is thick and demanding and addresses us honestly in our unsolved complexity.
- Such a preacher knows that whatever sustainable joy will be had in the historical process will not offer ease, comfort, or convenience but will come from trustworthy fidelity that withstands the challenges of hard times. Thus the "I am with you" of the God of the text and the "I am with you" of the community around this text turn out to yield the only joy that comes in this body of death where we find ourselves.
- Such a preacher knows that the world is filled with threat, danger, and risk, and current talk of "Security" serves mainly to keep us on Orange Alert and inured to the follies of the national security state. The only safety on offer is the embrace of attentive compassion that summons us and calls us by name.

I underscore these deep difficulties with the narrative in order to appreciate the risk of staking our lives on this narrative account of reality. The same difficulties, on a different scale, are a part of life as staked on the dominant reality. But that dominant narrative practice is rarely called to justify itself as is the narrative of the Gospel. Thus the prophetic preacher, with acute sensitivity for pastoral care, is always adjudicating these matters with honest and personal uneasiness.

- In that ancient world, the adherents to this narrative account of the world had to make the case that the YHWH narrative was more adequate than the claims of Canaanite religion, even while fools in their midst continued to say in their heart, "There is no God" (Ps. 14:1). Or better, without such scandalous dismissal, a different kind of denial, "The Lord will not do good, nor will he do harm" (Zeph. 1:12).
- In the world of the early church, the preachers had to make the case that the narrative of crucifixion-resurrection was a more

adequate account of reality, while the official religious leaders, allied with the dominant narrative of the empire, mocked him derisively: "In the same way the chief priests also, along with the scribes and elders, were mocking him, saying, 'He saved others; he cannot save himself. He is the King of Israel; let him come down from the cross now, and we will believe in him. He trusts in God; let God deliver him now, if he wants to; for he said, "I am God's Son."' The bandits who were crucified with him also taunted him in the same way" (Matt. 27:41-44).

• And now the case is yet to be made again for the narrative of emancipation and covenant wrought by an Agent who looks suspect according to the way of the world. The context in which that advocacy is to be made is one in which the dominant narrative is failing before our eyes. The inability of our strong military to have its way in the world, the inability of our strong economy to maintain its strength, perhaps the Gulf oil spill as an icon of a failed narrative of technological self-sufficiency, all together produce an endless round of anxiety that the world guaranteed by that dominant narrative is vanishing while we watch. Consequently, we live in an ocean of anxiety that is now scarcely bearable.

We are, for the most part, double-minded.[38] There is hidden deep within most of us, I suspect, a profound tension between these narratives, knowing better than to trust the dominant narrative but having a huge stake in its being true, wanting the gospel narrative to be true but reluctant to speak another language about the world other than the one in which we are palpably invested. It is the hard work of prophetic preaching, I propose, to make that tension explicit, available, and visible in order to permit informed, knowing choices. The reason it is such hard work is that the people with whom we do ministry, in their anxiety, have a huge stake in denial and keeping the tension hidden. And we ourselves share in that hope of keeping the tension hidden, because when it is acknowledged, we are held accountable for the work that is to be done and the decisions that are to be made. Prophetic preaching does not put people in crisis. Rather it names and makes palpable the crisis already pulsing among us. It is for that reason that we have such energy for resistance and denial. The hard work of adjudicating between these narratives is itself energizing. The hard work, in fact, is to keep the tension hidden, work that keeps us exhausted. Peter Berger describes the work of truthfulness as the process through which persons "switch worlds."[39] That has been the work since the ancient slaves "switched worlds" from that of pharaoh—the world of "cries"—to be the world of YHWH, where there was dancing and singing, "free at last." The summons of Deuteronomy, the script behind the prophets, is always to "choose," to "choose life," to "choose this day whom you will serve" (Josh. 24:15). Such redeciding is the quintessential human task, and we engaged in ministry of Word and Sacrament are the ones given access to that troubled possibility.

CHAPTER 2

Prophetic Preaching as Sustained, Disciplined, Emancipated Imagination

WHEN I PUBLISHED MY BOOK *The Prophetic Imagination* in 1978, I laid out a series of theses that voiced my fundamental understanding of Israel's prophets.[1] That series of theses continues to ring true, I believe. In this foray, I will reflect on those theses and hope to advance the argument a bit. I proposed:

- That the prophets in ancient Israel addressed the *royal consciousness* concerning the Jerusalem establishment and offered *a covenantal alternative* to that consciousness.
- That the Old Testament prophets had as their work a sustained *critique* of royal consciousness and the *energizing* of an alternative community.

I believe that these theses continue to be valid and are immediately pertinent to our own reflection on contemporary prophetic preaching.

I

But here I want to reflect on the title of that book, "Prophetic Imagination." In fact the title was rather happenstance at the end of the process of publication.

It was, nevertheless, a fortuitous formulation, for it juxtaposed the notion of "prophetic" with its freight of earnest ethical urgency with the term "imagination" that was, at the time, not much in vogue among interpreters. The juxtaposition of the two terms, of course, redefined each of them. To qualify "prophetic" by "imagination" is to dig deeper than moral earnestness into the notion of playful, venturesome probing into the unknown that requires poetic utterance and that evokes daring images and metaphors, all in the service of an elusiveness out beyond royal totalism. To evade royal totalism requires an emancipated imagination that refuses the domesticated categories of settled control.

On the other hand, to qualify the term "imagination" by the adjective "prophetic" delivers imagination from sheer fantasy into a world of covenantal engagement that features YHWH as the compelling partner of both the human prophetic utterer and those who heard the prophetic utterance in serious ways. Thus the word pair identifies an elusive, daring, subversive verbal probe in ancient Israel that intended to subvert the settled political, economic order of royal Jerusalem. That subversion was based upon the character of YHWH who is the key agent in the sub-version of reality that Israel tells in its normative narrative. It turned out, after the accidental juxtaposition of the terms, some years after publication, that I discovered that Flannery O'Connor, in one of her letters, used the same juxtaposition of terms. That of course fits just right, for O'Connor was always preoccupied with subverting settled reality and did so with a religious nuance. Thus there can be no doubt that the ancient prophets of Israel would have found a ready ally in O'Connor. She, like them, utilized daring utterance to displace old truisms that were trusted far too much.

It is on the basis of that juxtaposition of "prophetic" and "imagination" that I consider prophetic preaching. It is easy enough to imagine that Amos, commonly regarded as the first of the great prophets in Israel, appeared de novo with his shrill, playful, elusive poetic utterance. For as he himself said,

> The lion has roared;
> who will not fear?
> The Lord GOD has spoken;
> who can but prophesy? (Amos 3:8)

His utterance, moreover, was enough to see him banished from the royal capital of Samaria: "And Amaziah said to Amos, 'O seer, go, flee away to the land of Judah, earn your bread there, and prophesy there; but never again prophesy at Bethel, for it is the king's sanctuary, and it is a temple of the kingdom'" (Amos 7:12-13). De novo as he may have appeared (and in fact we do not know), that is not the way Israel remembers the matter, contrary to much critical judgment. For the canonical shape of "the law and the prophets" provides antecedents to Amos and his fellow subversives. The way the canon works, the antecedent narrative had already prepared, presented, and witnessed to the irascible, wonder-working God of the Torah. This God is waiting for the chance to reemerge in Israel after the stifling reductionism of the royal consciousness accented by Solomon.[2] This waiting God is the one who called the world into being, who worked an impossibility for Sarah and her ilk, who overwhelmed pharaoh on behalf of emancipation, who sent meat, water, and bread from who knows where; this God spoke ten times at Sinai and summoned Israel in covenant to an either/or of life or death, blessing or curse. We have seen in Deuteronomy 34, at the end of the Torah, that Moses and his belated exilic contemporaries are waiting for what comes next from YHWH. It turns out that YHWH is also waiting. YHWH is waiting restlessly, at the end of the royal consciousness, lurking in the pages of the canon, waiting to reemerge, to reappear, to be reuttered in thickness. The Torah is waiting for the prophets, and the God of the Torah is waiting for the utterance of the prophets who have the old script in front of them. And when the prophets speak, they do so imaginatively; they voice "prophetic imagination," and YHWH is played into the midst of royal history as an awkward misfit who does not accommodate the ancient regime. YHWH reemerges in metaphor and in image, in poem and in oracle.

Thus I return to my thesis stated earlier:

> Prophetic preaching is an effort to imagine the world as though
> YHWH, the creator of heaven and earth, the Father of our Lord
> Jesus Christ whom we Christians name as Father, Son, and Spirit, is
> a real character and a defining agent in the world.

That effort with fresh contemporaneity, moreover, is rooted, according to my derivative thesis, in a normative narrative memory: prophetic preaching is an act of imagination that is propelled and funded by the previous acts of imagination in the normative story of Israel that evokes YHWH as defining character and agent. Thus YHWH recruits Amos (and his ilk that follow) to dare the right words. Or if you prefer, Amos and his company wait on YHWH to generate words, the utterance of which will put the known world at risk. Thus we are dealing, as we always are in this thick traditioning process, with at least a double layer of imagination if not more:

- There is a remembered construal of reality that is the baseline offered, for example, in the "credo" of Deuteronomy 26. That remembered construal exhibits YHWH in all of YHWH's elusive, irascible freedom that refuses to submit to royal consciousness.
- There is an ancient contemporary construal of reality by the prophets that is funded by that remembered construal of reality.
- And then, belatedly, we may imagine ourselves, as prophetic preachers, offering yet another layer of imagination. There is our own contemporary construal in which we utter the world of YHWH in a context of our present royal consciousness that seeks to domesticate everything with its totalizing management.

It is clear that without *the remembered construal* of the Torah, *the ancient contemporary construal* of reality and *our own contemporary construal* of reality make little sense and sound like a cranky rhetorical fling.

We may see, for example, that Martin Luther King, surely a prophet among us, speaks fresh utterance. But his fresh subversive utterance is shot through with ancient imagination. Thus, "I have a dream" surely appeals to and is grounded in the ancient promises of the old prophets that in turn are grounded in the ancient covenantal blessings and the lyric of creation in which all will finally be "very good," as the creator has intended from the outset. King's final utterance, "I have been to the mountaintop," could not have been said so powerfully if Martin had not stood with Moses at the awesomeness of Sinai and "gazed" on God (Exod. 24:11, Feiler) or if Martin had not stood with Moses in Deuteronomy 34 looking into the land of promise, or if Martin had not been alongside Isaiah when he was commanded to "Get you up to a high mountain" (Isa. 40:9).[3] King is a clear and dramatic embodiment of the way in which the tradition is layered and layered again with the thick voicing of YHWH who keeps uttering, even in the face of determined royal silencing of such speech.

II

Thus I propose that the ancient prophets are in fact *imaginers*; and those of us who follow in their wake are *imaginers* after them. That does not mean that the prophets have no interest in ethical questions or in historical realities. Of course not! It does mean, however, that ethical analysis by itself will never adequately discern what the prophets are doing because their ethical concern is regularly rearticulated and reformulated according to image and metaphor that sober ethical reflection does not countenance. It does mean that our attempts to replicate prophetic utterance in our historical-critical, "objective" way will never echo what is given in these utterances.

By "imagination" I mean the capacity to generate and enunciate images of reality that are not rooted in the world in front of us. Thus imagination moves outside the box of the given and the taken for granted. As Paul Ricoeur has seen, the parables of Jesus are a classic example of such an act of imagination.[4] In his parables Jesus entertained a world other than the one assumed by his listeners. Ricoeur calls the parables "limit expressions" that push outside the familiar to open up unexplored and unrecognized territory in the space between YHWH and the listening community. It is obvious at the outset that such emancipated, subversive utterance contradicts and flies in the face of much of our critical work that has offered "explanations" for everything in the prophets according to Enlightenment rationality. But prophetic utterance, under the discipline of the Torah, erupts in emotive possibility that is not constrained by our reasonableness. The prophets work with and keep expanding a large inventory of images and metaphors that are concrete, so that we can sense the urgent impact of a "heated oven" (Hos. 7:4-7), or a "dove, silly and without sense" (Hos. 7:11), or a calf to be kissed (Hos. 13:2), or "a cake not turned" (Hos. 7:8), or a vine with pitiful grapes (Isa. 5:2, 4), or a broken cistern (Jer. 2:13), or a desperate prostitute (Jer. 4:30), or a "drop from a bucket" (Isa. 40:15), or a fearless worm (Isa. 41:14), or, or, or . . . The images are concretely resonant with the real, situated life of Israel in the world. They are, at the same time, slightly removed, in their edgy way, from didactic specificity about public issues.

It is of immense importance, and not often enough fully appreciated, that the prophets characteristically spoke in poetic cadences. This is not to suggest that all poetry is prophetic. It is to suggest, rather, that the characteristic prophetic utterance intends to evoke, to shock, to tease, to play, to probe, not with certitude but with possibility for what has been, until now, unthinkable and unsayable. I have elsewhere suggested that prophetic utterance is not unlike the fastball of Bob Gibson, the great pitcher of the St. Louis Cardinals.[5] Of such pitches, the commentators say that they "pop," they "move," they "surge," they surprise, they overwhelm. Such utterance staggers and offends among the listeners. But it also opens vistas of possibility where we had not thought to go and where in fact, we are most reluctant to go. Such evocation challenges and emancipates in ways that linear prose could never do, for the world is offered at fresh angle. And of course, it is even more so if we keep in mind that the odd utterance is said to be given by YHWH, thus YHWH's own image or metaphor or nuance or hyperbole or contradiction.

In such performance, this restless utterer refuses to conform to or accept the safe world of royal administration.

Such imagination, grounded in narrative imagination that attests YHWH, is in competition with other imaginations that are on offer. That these other imaginations are being contested by prophetic imagination is often implied rather than made explicit, but it is always in contest.

In the ancient world of Israel, the dominant imagination was formidable and aggressively public:

- It imagined David and his entourage with a perpetual, unconditional promise from YHWH. (2 Sam. 7:10-16)
- It imagined that the temple in Jerusalem was to be YHWH's permanent habitat, a claim given frequent liturgical reiteration. (1 Kgs. 8:12-13)
- It imagined Israel's exceptionalism as YHWH's chosen people, not subject to the restrains of history. (Deut. 7:6)

These several claims, enunciated *in oracle* (2 Sam. 7:1-16), *in liturgical declaration* (1 Kgs. 8:12-13), and *in sermon* (Deut. 7:6), gave a basis for public life in Jerusalem, a basis that prophetic imagination took to be phony, misleading, and ultimately lethal. That "world in front of us" had immense power in its articulation, an articulation seemingly matched and confirmed by the technology and hardware of durability.[6]

In like manner, the "world in front to us" in contemporary US society has immense power, as it is carried variously by slogans, mantras, and various historical illusions. Thus variously the dominant imagination of the national security state trades on

- "A city set on a hill,"
- "Land of the free and home of the brave,"
- "Don't tread on me,"
- "Leader of the free world,"
- "White man's burden,"
- "Manifest destiny."

All of these mantras, and many more that could be added, amount to a claim of exceptionalism that readily melds "God" into "country." That melding, moreover, justifies macho violence in the world on behalf of "democratic capitalism." As any preacher will attest, the political-theological force of this imagination is immense and resists challenge, its devotees being acutely vigilant to spot any hint of challenge.

The claim of dominant imagination, in both ancient Israel and in contemporary US "democratic capitalism," is a totalizing claim that does not permit any reality or any claim outside of its regime and certainly does not welcome any rival claim. This judgment can be tested by asking any would-be prophetic preacher to identify the topics that cannot be mentioned in church. The list of them reflects the totalizing exceptionalism that is given religious sanction and that seeks to silence any question about that claim.

III

Thus prophetic preaching, ancient or contemporary, is in a contest of competing imaginations—a contest between old Torah imagination that features YHWH as character and agent and the dominant imagination that predictably assimilates God into its powerful socio-political claims. I have gotten clear about this context of imaginations from the final pages of *Torture and Eucharist* by William Cavanaugh, who narrates the way in which the totalizing regime of Augusto Pinochet in Chile sustained itself and silenced all alternatives by fear, intimidation, and torture.[7] But then, Cavanaugh reports, the Roman Catholic bishops in Chile—albeit, sadly, belatedly—awoke to the crisis of society and appealed to eucharistic imagination to counter the dominant imagination of the totalizing regime of Pinochet.

Cavanaugh concludes his study with reference to a novel of Lawrence Thornton, *Imagining Argentina*, in which the lead character, Carlos Rueda, imagines, by his stories, an alternative Argentina outside the reach of the totalizing regime. In the novel, Carlos does not confront tanks with stories, but

> rightly grasps that the contest is not between imagination and the real, but between two types of imagination, that of the generals and that of their opponents. The nightmare world of the torture and disappearance of bodies is inseparable from the generals' imagination of what Argentina and Argentines are. Carlos realizes that 'he was being dreamed by [General] Guzman and the others, that he has been living inside their imagination.[8]

Carlos attests, "We have to believe in the power of imagination because it is all we have, and ours is stronger than theirs."[9] In the end, "Carlos's imagination is manifested in real effects; escaping the imagination of the state means that bodies go free. The imagination is defined as nothing less than 'the magnificent cause of being.'"[10] Cavanaugh comments on the novel: "To participate in the Eucharist is to live inside God's imagination. It is to be caught up into what is really real, the body of Christ."[11] It is the bite of the prophetic tradition that it can out-imagine the dominant imagination, because it is in sync with the truth of YHWH and because it touches the bodily reality of life that the dominant imagination must, perforce, disregard. The intersection of *YHWH* and *bodily reality* is already narrated in the old tradition in Exodus 2:23-25, where the cry of bodily pain evoked YHWH, and in the prophetic tradition in Jeremiah 22:15-16, wherein caring for the poor is to know YHWH. This way of voicing YHWH lives very close to the reality of bodily pain and so to bodily reality.

It is a tall order, of course, to think that the prophets could out-imagine the Jerusalem establishment. To be sure, such a prophetic practice in ancient Israel was fragile and vulnerable. As the history of Jerusalem moved closer to its termination as a Judean state, however, the prophet Jeremiah discovered that he had unexpected allies and eventually is even sought out by the frightened king who at least recognized that the tale of unconditional exceptionalism had failed (Jer. 37:17). The tradition of Jeremiah attests that there were in the Jerusalem power structure people who knew better and who thought differently when they could risk such thinking to attest that the dominant narrative had failed.[12]

The prophets in ancient Israel refused the dominant narrative. Their standing ground for that refusal is simply, "Thus saith the LORD." They claimed to have been given an alternative word that called them to a different utterance. They claimed to be in touch with a more reliable truth. But of course all such claims are unproveable; all that is available is the utterance. In their utterance,

- They do not accept the Davidic claim of unconditional divine endorsement, for they imagine YHWH as an adversary of the city;
- They do not accept Jerusalem as the perpetual habitat of YHWH, for they imagine that YHWH will absent YHWH's self from the temple;
- They do not accept the ultimate claim of exceptionalism, for they imagine that YHWH will come against the city and its ideological posturing.

They imagine against establishment imagination. It would be, *mutatis mutandis*, as though a prophetic poet in our time imagined outside the totalizing ideology of our national security state:

- Such an act of imagination would not accept the absolute claims of democratic capitalism, especially in its current skewed form.

- Such an act of imagination would not accept the litany of military consumerism with its limitless self-indulgence and sense of entitlement.

All of that requires of us the capacity to think and speak *mutatis mutandis*!

IV

Prophetic participation in the contests of imaginations is not simply to negate dominant imagination and to expose it as flawed. Beyond that, these poetic utterers dared to propose an alternative shape for reality that is offered in a "scale of relationship" in which YHWH is the other party as a real participant and agent. Thus the appeal to "relationship" drew from the old pattern of covenant and contradicts the reductionism of the royal consciousness that had precluded the categories of relationship that bespeak vulnerability, freedom, passion, and mutual responsibility. In their recovery and rearticulation of the world of relationship, the prophets engaged in daring imagination.

1. They imagine familial relationships of husband-wife and parent-child:

> And I will take you for my wife forever; I will take you for my wife in righteousness and in justice, in steadfast love, and in mercy. I will take you for my wife in faithfulness; and you shall know the Lord. (Hos. 2:19-20)

> Can a girl forget her ornaments,
>   or a bride her attire?
> Yet my people have forgotten me,
>   days without number. (Jer. 2:32)

> I thought you would call me, My Father,
>   and would not turn from following me.
> Instead, as a faithless wife leaves her husband,
>   so you have been faithless to me, O house of Israel,
>   says the Lord. (Jer. 3:19-20)

> But you trusted in your beauty, and played the whore because of your fame, and lavished your whorings on any passer-by. . . . therefore, I will gather all your lovers, with whom you took pleasure, all those you loved and all those you hated; I will gather them against

> you from all around, and will uncover your nakedness to them, so
> that they may see all your nakedness. (Ezek. 16:15, 37)

The rhetoric is not "applied" in any direct way to current social issues.
Rather the rhetoric serves to change the subject, to insist that there is a more
urgent agenda than the one taken on by the royal imagination.

2. They imagine power relations of YHWH as king, judge, shepherd,
warrior—images taken from actual public life in Israel.[13] Only now the terms
are reassigned, away from would-be kings and would-be judges, now assigned
to the real ruler and to the dismissal of the pretenders:

> In the year that King Uzziah died, I saw the Lord sitting on a throne,
> high and lofty . . . (Isa. 6:1)

> The LORD rises to argue his case;
>   he stands to judge the peoples.
> The LORD enters into judgment
>   with the elders and princes of his people;
> It is you who have devoured the vineyard;
>   the spoil of the poor is in your houses.
> What do you mean by crushing my people,
>   by grinding the face of the poor? says the Lord GOD of hosts.
>   (Isa. 3:13-15)

> Ah, you shepherds of Israel who have been feeding yourselves!
> Should not shepherds feed the sheep? You eat the fat, you clothe
> yourselves with the wool, you slaughter the fatlings; but you do not
> feed the sheep. You have not strengthened the weak, you have not
> healed the sick, you have not bound up the injured, you have not
> brought back the strayed, you have not sought the lost . . . I myself
> will search for my sheep . . . (Ezek. 34:2-4, 11)

3. The relational accent of the prophets eschews the more convenient
categories of omnipotence, omnipresence, and omniscience. It may be that
those capacities are all implied concerning YHWH. But that is not how the
prophets speak of YHWH. These categories, no doubt preferred in dominant
imagination, are subverted by interrelational categories that exhibit passion
and engagement, and that entertain possibilities not yet in hand.

4. The prophets dismiss the pursuit of commodities and the practice of "the
good life" of endless consumption:

Alas for those who lie on beds of ivory,
　　and lounge on their couches,
and eat lambs from the flock,
　　and calves from the stall;
who sing idle songs to the sound of the harp,
　　and like David improvise on instruments of music;
who drink wine from bowls,
　　and anoint themselves with finest oils . . . (Amos 6:4-6)

They see that such avarice leads to skewed social relationships in society, and eventually to the abuse of the neighbor:

Hear this word . . .
who oppress the poor, who crush the needy,
　　who say to their husbands, "Bring something to drink!"
　　(Amos 4:1)

Ah, you who join house to house,
　　who add field to field,
until there is room for none but you,
　　And you are left to live alone
　　in the midst of the land! (Isa. 5:8)

They covet fields, and seize them;
　　houses, and take them away;
they oppress householder and house,
　　people and their inheritance. (Mic. 2:2)

5. The insistence upon relationships makes clear that the real issue in society is not wealth or scarcity or control. It is rather fidelity toward God and toward neighbor. Prophetic imagination begins in the ancient covenant; but it is carried, in concrete articulation, to current issues of the day, so that daily transactions are delineated as instances of old covenantal commitments. In this accent upon relationship, prophetic imagination in effect delegitimates the dominant imagination that rushed past relationships in pursuit of control. The point everywhere voiced by the prophets is summarized by Jeremiah: "Thus says the LORD: Do not let the wise boast in their wisdom, do not let mighty boast in their might, do not let the wealthy boast in their wealth; but let those who boast boast in this, that they understand and know me, that I am the LORD; I act with steadfast love, justice, and righteousness in the earth,

for in these things I delight, says the LORD" (Jer. 9:23-24). The double triad of *wisdom, might, wealth* and *steadfast love, justice, righteousness* states the deep either/or that the dominant narrative did not want or acknowledge in ancient Jerusalem. The task of prophetic imagination is to find compelling ways to portray the crisis of society that is missed or disregarded in the dominant imagination. That crisis variously consists in

- *loyalty or betrayal* while the dominant imagination is preoccupied with utilitarian and contractual arrangements;
- *fidelity or infidelity* while the dominant culture works by coercion and manipulation;
- *obedience or disobedience* while the dominant narrative assumes there is no accountability beyond self-interest;
- *trust or fear* while the dominant narrative teaches that we must trust none and fear all;
- *truth or denial* while the dominant narrative does not believe there is truthfulness that outruns self-interest;
- *hope or despair* while the dominant narrative attests that we are in a zero-sum game with no new gifts to be given;
- *life or death* while the dominant narrative simply imagines a return to "normalcy."

Such relational categories that inform prophetic imagination cannot be reduced to a program or a syllogism or a blueprint or a memo. Rather such categories require poetic ambiguity, elusive playfulness, always being under way and in negotiation, ready always to be surprised. Thus the contrast is not only in *the content* of these imaginations but also in *the modes of imagining*, for prophetic imagination always offers yet another utterance and refuses closure and absolutism, the very modes in which dominant imagination specializes.

V

Contemporary prophetic imagination, as it joins issue with dominant imagination, is continually funded by remembered imagination:

1. Prophetic imagination is rooted in the *doxologies of creation*. Consequently, it moves from the gift of abundance that is ordained in creation, a sure sense that a viable, sustainable food chain is offered in generosity but can be placed in acute jeopardy by exploitation of creation. That jeopardy leads to

an imagined scenario of the destruction of creation, even while we debate the environmental crisis:

> I looked on the earth, and lo, it was waste and void;
>> and to the heavens, and they had no light.
> I looked on the mountains and lo, they were quaking,
>> and all the hills moved to and fro.
> I looked, and lo, there was no one at all,
>> and all the birds of the air had fled.
> I looked, and lo, the fruitful land was desert,
>> and all its cities were laid in ruins
>> before the Lord, before his fierce anger. (Jer. 4:23-26)

The termination of creation, the recall of grain, wine, wool, and flax (Hos. 2:9), however, does not preclude a new wave of fruitful creation granted by the mercy of God (Hos. 2:21-22). Such prophetic imagination can critique practices and resist policies (such as war policies) that inevitably abuse creation and disrupt fruitfulness. There is no doubt that dominant imagination, characteristically, is premised on an assumption of scarcity and so does not allow for the generous capacity of the creator to give gifts of life.

2. Contemporary prophetic imagination is rooted in *the ancestral narratives of new birth* (new rebirth) that is given just as the human subject reaches its end in barrenness. It recognizes that birth is the most elemental miracle of creation and of human history, and knows that the endless recital of "begets" in the genealogies of ancient Israel constitutes an inventory of miracles by which the world works. The old story of birth is continually retold, because there is the gift of new life, of birth and rebirth, beyond self-sufficiency. Thus in the depth of exile, the poet can reach back to mother Sarah for new possibility:

> Sing, O barren one who did not bear;
>> burst into song and shout,
>> you who have not been in labor!
> For the children of the desolate woman will be more
>> than the children of her that is married, says the Lord.
> Enlarge the site of your tent,
>> and let the curtains of your habitations be stretched out;
> do not hold back; lengthen your cords
>> and strengthen your stakes.
> For you will spread out to the right and to the left,

and your descendants will possess the nations
and will settle the desolate towns. (Isa. 54:1-3)

3. Contemporary prophetic imagination is rooted in the memory of *the exodus deliverance* that features emancipation from the pharaonic system of coercion. Such emancipation is inexplicable, but the prophets continue to bear witness to just such a contemporary deliverance. Thus the exodus memory becomes a way to speak about homecoming from the empire: "Therefore, the days are surely coming, says the LORD, when it shall no longer be said, 'As the LORD lives who brought the house of Israel up out of the land of Egypt,' but 'As the LORD lives who brought out and led the offspring of the house of Israel out of the land of the north and out of all the lands where he had driven them.' Then they shall live in their own land" (Jer. 23:7-8).

Do not remember the former things,
    or consider the things of old.
I am about to do a new thing;
    now it springs forth, do you not perceive it?
I will make a way in the wilderness
    and rivers in the desert. (Isa. 43:18-19)

Matthew, moreover, introduces his narrative of Jesus through a quote from Hosea 11:1 in order to show that Jesus is situated in the same narrative of the deliverance wrought by the God of the Exodus: "Then Joseph got up, took the child and his mother by night, and went to Egypt, and remained there until the death of Herod. This was to fulfill what had been spoken by the Lord through the prophet, 'Out of Egypt I have called my son'" (Matt. 2:14-15). It is no wonder that the Exodus narrative keeps reappearing, even in the US account of emancipation.[14] The end of apartheid in South Africa, moreover, cannot be understood in any way except as an Exodus.

4. Contemporary prophetic imagination is rooted in *the liturgical reiteration of Sinai* in which the covenant is remembered and reenacted in each new generation: "Not with our ancestors did the LORD make this covenant, but with us, who are all of us here alive today" (Deut. 5:3). The interpretive task in ancient Israel (and the ongoing work of Judaism) is to attend to the commandments of Sinai in order that they should be relevant and compelling in each new generation in each new circumstance. The claim of Sinai is that a proper way of life is in obedience to the God of Sinai. The tradition, of course, has tough going in the face of Enlightenment autonomy that focuses on pragmatic reason without any ultimate accountability. Michael Fishbane,

however, has eloquently made the case that the disciplines of Torah function to keep the faithful "mindful" of the reality of God at the center of life.[15] That mindfulness, moreover, is an antidote to and resistance against the "mindlessness" that besets life lived by dominant narrative. Mindless autonomy, as we are able to see, does not foster a viable, sustainable social infrastructure.

It is not a surprise that interpretive work on the commandments in present day should evoke deep and serious dispute. Of course! No one in the traditioning process ever thought that transition from ancient narrative to contemporary life would be easy or obvious. That serious dispute, especially concerning sexuality and economics, is a dispute in prophetic imagination about how to answer the God of Sinai. It is not a discussion of autonomy or being able to have life on our own terms.

In the prophetic corpus there are many allusions to the Torah commandments.[16] Only twice is the Decalogue explicitly cited. In Hosea 4:1-2, contemporary Israel in the eighth century is indicted for violating the commandments: "There is no faithfulness or loyalty, and no knowledge of God in the land. Swearing, lying, and murder, and stealing and adultery break out; bloodshed follows bloodshed." The "therefore" that follows in verse 3 affirms that the destruction of creation follows from disobedience of Torah. In Jeremiah 7:9, the Decalogue is cited with the anticipated punishment of forfeiture of the city and the land. The prophets entertain no simple, crude supernaturalism; nonetheless they do think again about the requirements and limits of a sustainable creation or, more specifically, about a sustainable community in the land of promise. We have in recent time, in our society, been on a binge of self-indulgence, imagining that "anything goes." But from time to time, the facts on the ground catch up with the ancient Torah teaching, and we come face to face with the restraint, limit, and accountability that cannot be abrogated.

5. The tradition of Deuteronomy, the fullest theology of covenant in the Old Testament, has taken the requirements of Sinai and has codified them into a rigorous quid pro quo of blessing and curse. Such an articulation is old fashioned and may readily put to ignoble, authoritarian use. The rigor of covenant, however, is an act of imagination that intended to counter the complacency of dominant tradition. Indeed, it is easy enough to see that the Torah interpretation of Deuteronomy is a self-conscious counter to the foolish self-aggrandizement that swirls around the memory of Solomon.[17] The prophetic appeal to the quid pro quo of Deuteronomy and its covenantal insistences is not excessively crude or coercive. Thus the oracle cited in Hosea 4 is poetry, and the teaching in Jeremiah is sermonic. They are insistences that the old tradition is still a truthteller, because it attests to the Lord of the covenant as a present force in the life of Israel.

6. Contemporary prophetic imagination is informed by *the terminal narrative of Deuteronomy 34*. That imagination knows about waiting. It knows about having forfeited, like Moses, entry into God's new promise of land. It knows about the caesura of disappointment. It offers utterance about a pot that cannot be mended (Jer. 19:11), about a vineyard that will be rooted up (Isa. 5:1-7), about a coming wailing in loss (Amos 8:1; Mic. 2:4; Jer. 9:17-19). The space between Deuteronomy and Joshua at the Jordan, between Torah and Prophets, between Moses and Joshua is a dread waiting. Isaiah can line it out:

> For a brief moment I abandoned you,
> but with great compassion I will gather you.
> In overflowng wrath for a moment
> I hid my face from you,
> but with everlasting love I will have compassion on you,
> says the LORD, your Redeemer. (Isa. 54:7-8)

The wait has been "for a moment." But the moment endures. And then, beyond the dread, there is a fresh wave of divine compassion and everlasting love. The dominant narrative will not and cannot wait. It believes in instant demand and instant delivery, that there should be no delay.

Prophetic imagination is committed to two propositions: (a) *The remembered imagination* of Torah is powerfully contemporary in new time and place; (b) *Contemporary imagination* funded by *remembered imagination* offers a critique of *dominant imagination* and offers an alternative construal of reality that is life giving. Thus in every elusive utterance given by this elusive God of the tradition, the gift of life is mediated outside the totalizing claims of dominant imagination.

So we are thus able to reflect on the tasks of prophetic imagination:

1. That task in the eighth century BCE—in a remarkable procession of Amos, Hosea, Micah, and Isaiah—was to bring contemporary life under the aegis of the old tradition and the God of that tradition. The prophets spouted oracles concerning justice and fidelity that are known to be the norm for covenant; they assert that the urban-culture of Samaria in the North and Jerusalem in the South was in profound violation of the covenant and was to receive the outcomes of violation that in the old covenant structure was curse. Thus Amos 4:6-11 offers a recital of curses, in turn famine (v. 6), drought (vv. 7-8), blight, mildew, and locust (v. 9), pestilence (v. 10), and even earthquake (v. 11). The recital of curses, in a way characteristic for prophetic oracle, comes to the "therefore" of verse 12 that is reinforced by the doxology of

verse 13, which affirms that the creator God can indeed wield the forces of creation in the enforcement of covenant. As the canon has it, the prophets who critique the urban-royal-priestly culture with its sense of entitlement and it ethical obduracy are vindicated by the destruction of the two states and the two capitol cities. It was, of course, possible to understand and explain these destructions in other ways. In the context of the old Torah narrative, however, this connection between covenant violation and covenant consequence is a compelling and inescapable conclusion.

2. The prophetic voices of the sixth century BCE had a very different task. After the destruction of Jerusalem and the deep grief of Israel that came to the edge of despair, the prophets of that era of demise and deportation had to address the despair. They did so with an offer of hope for a new social possibility, namely, the return to the homeland and the restoration of a flourishing Jerusalem.[18] With a rich variety of images, they anticipated restoration—Isaiah with a restored David (Isa. 11:1-9; see Amos 9:11; Hosea 3:5), Jeremiah with a restored covenant (31:31-34), Ezekiel with a restored temple (40–48), and even the completed tradition of Amos with an anticipation of a revived creation (9:12-14).

In order to articulate these promises, the prophets must, perforce, appeal to a very different part of the old tradition than did their antecedents in the eighth and seventh centuries. Now there is no accent on the quid pro quo of the covenant structure. Rather there is appeal to the divine promises to Abraham and the derivative promise to David. Now the future depends on the free gift of YHWH that will be given, even in the face of Israel's recalcitrance.[19] YHWH will enact a *novum* in world history that will be commensurate with the inexplicable *novum* of the birth of Isaac, or of the emancipation from Egypt, or the bread from heaven. This aspect of prophetic preaching is not often in purview among us. Clearly the final form of the prophetic tradition will no more countenance the *despair* of the displaced covenant members than it would earlier accept the *denial* of complacent covenant members.

The full play of the old tradition, as voiced by the prophets, concerns both *the rigorous conditionality of Sinai* and *the astonishing unconditionality of Abraham (and David)*. The prophetic enterprise cannot do without both of these accents, the problem being when to sound which note. Thus Ronald Clements, in assessing the canonical shape of the prophetic tradition, concludes that both judgment and hope belong properly to the truth-telling, hope-telling of the prophets:

> In such fashion we can at least come to understand the value and meaning of the way in which distinctive patterns have been imposed

on the prophetic collections of the canon so that warnings of doom and disaster are always followed by promises of hope and restoration. . . . Ultimately the final result in the prophetic corpus of the canon formed a recognizable unity not entirely dissimilar from that of the Pentateuch . . . the Former and Latter Prophets, comprising the various preserved prophecies of a whole series of inspired individuals, acquired an overarching thematic unity. This centered on the death and rebirth of Israel, interpreted theologically as acts of divine judgment and salvation.[20]

3. There are no direct, obvious, or easy moves to be made from ancient utterance to contemporary prophetic preaching. Nevertheless the prophetic tradition is both a resource and an instruction for our own prophetic preaching which is, as I propose, testimony to the cruciality of YHWH in the public scene. Without reference to YHWH, there was no reason to critique the denial of eighth-century Jerusalem. Without reference to YHWH, there was no ground in the sixth century to break the despair in an act of hope. Without YHWH, Jerusalem and then the displaced of Israel could go their way in denial and then despair, except of course the prophets insisted otherwise.

And now in our twenty-first century, we in the United States are, I believe, in a strange mix of *denial and despair.* In our denial, we keep imagining that it will all "work out" and that the failure of our society is not as deep or long term as we might suspect. In our despair, we have the sinking feeling that there will be no return to a previous well-being, and we are left in a bad place about long-term prospects.

In that situation of *denial* that pretends it will all work out and *of despair* that suspects it will not work out, the old tradition of YHWH as the God who enforces covenant and the God who gives newness lurks in prophetic utterance waiting to be mobilized. It is the work of twenty-first century prophetic preachers, is it not, to name the denial and to identify the infidelities that make our common life toxic. It is the work of twenty-first century prophetic preachers, is it not, to name the despair and witness to the divine resolve for newness that may break the vicious cycles of self-destruction and make new common life possible.

Such utterance that names the denial we prefer and names the despair we embrace is an awkward, unwelcome act. Who wants to hear that? Or who wants to say that? But it has ever been so. Prophets characteristically utter what jars against established imagination. Thus Karl Barth, in his exposition of the strangeness and newness of the Bible, can say: "We have found in the Bible a new world, God, God's sovereignty, God's glory, God's incomprehensible love. Not the history of man but the history of God! Not the virtues of men but the virtues of him who hath called us out of darkness into his marvelous light! Not human standpoints but the standpoint of God!"[21] Nowhere is that new world of the Holy God more evident than in the prophetic utterances, especially in the face of dominant imagination that imagines a "history of man" on our own.[22] Prophetic preaching is dangerous work, not only because it has a subversive edge but because it requires an epistemological break with the assumed world of dominant imagination. This epistemological break makes us aware of our assumptions we have not recognized or reflected upon. It is that epistemological break that caused Pharaoh to say:

> "Who is the LORD, that I should heed him and let Israel go? I do not know the LORD, and I will not let Israel go." (Exod. 5:2)

It is the same break that caused the celebration of David in Psalm 89 to end in dismayed query:

> Lord, where is your steadfast love of old,
>   which by your faithfulness you swore to David? (Ps. 89:49)

It is the same epistemological break that permitted the poet in grief to say:

> But this I call to mind,
>   and therefore I have hope:
> The steadfast love of the LORD never ceases,
>   his mercies never come to an end;
> they are new every morning;
>   great is your faithfulness. (Lam. 3:21-23)

It is the same epistemological break that allows Isaiah to say:

> Comfort, O comfort my people,
>   says your God.
> Speak tenderly to Jerusalem,
>   and cry to her
> that she has served her term,
>   that her penalty is paid,
> that she has received from the LORD's hand
>   double for all her sins. (Isa. 40:1-2)

Eventually, it is the same break that permits the church to exclaim:

Christ is risen!
He is risen indeed!

The world is reimagined!
Thus the challenge of prophetic preaching, which eschews trivial assurances of moral advice or theological precision or entertainment, has a harder task:

- How to imagine *a world of generosity* when the old parsimony has failed?
- How to imagine *a world of trusting relationships* when the tale of self-sufficient lives has grown cold?
- How to imagine *a turn toward emancipation* when we cower in resistance against any "departure" (exodus) from old safe places of compulsion?
- How to imagine *a life of generative obedience* after our presumed autonomy has turned out to be empty?
- How to imagine *a God who summons* after we have been glad to "come of age"?
- How to imagine *a long wait* at the river for entry into a new territory of promise when we are habituated in wanting it all now?

The prophetic act, now as always, is decidedly upstream and against the grain. Its work is to take deeply rooted memories (to which we still tip our hats in vague acknowledgment) and show how these memories continue to inform and shape and compel even now. It is an act that requires rereading contemporary context in the presence of YHWH, who is the subject of all our imaginings. Such a rereading must of course pay attention to "trends" and "emerging possibilities." More than that, it must do, as did these ancient utterers, a more serious social analysis that notices the interface between truth and power, and that is not distracted from the costs of bodily pain that are paid on behalf of those who live too well. Indeed, one could conclude that the entire trajectory of prophetic truth-telling is triggered by the divine utterance:

"I have observed the misery of my people who are in Egypt; I have heard their cry on account of their taskmasters. Indeed, I know their sufferings, and I have come down to deliver them from the Egyptians, and to bring them up out of that land to a good and broad land, a land flowing with milk and honey . . ." (Exod. 3:7-8)

The God of all gods is compelled by groan and cry (Exod. 2:23-24) and is mobilized on behalf of those who suffer. It is that cry that is the existential truth-telling that activates God and summons God's people.

VI

These conclusions about prophetic imagination occur to me:

1. The preaching venue is an arena for alternative imagination that owes nothing to dominant imagination. This act of alternative imagination is not authoritarian or excessively confrontational; at its best, it is genuinely interactive:

- It is interactive between preacher and congregation because both parties are situated in dominant imagination and yearn for otherwise.
- It is interactive between a presumed world that is held in common and a proposed world that is invariably new and strange for all of us.
- It is interactive between a remembered imagination to which we vaguely assent and a contemporary imagination that requires uncommon courage.

2. The work of prophetic preaching requires always emerging images and metaphors that are never simple reiteration. Like every agile rabbi, Jesus, in his parables, told new stories that gave fresh slant to reality and generated new possibility among those who heard him. His parables are indeed a mode of the prophetic, imagining new possibilities. In like manner, the Old Testament prophets do not simply reiterate but offer new images and new imagination that, when received and pondered, may take our breath away—just like when in a therapeutic conversation an obvious truth is spoken and becomes to us strange and new.

3. Prophetic utterance is offered in circumstance dictated by dominant imagination but is utterance that contradicts what is taken for granted. Such imagination refuses to accept accepted explanations for present circumstance. Thus,

- Prophetic imagination speaks of elemental jeopardy that is commonly explained away.
- Prophetic imagination exposes self-sufficiency as foolish self-deception.

- Prophetic imagination names the fear of emancipation that keeps us locked in to hopeless submissiveness.
- Prophetic imagination names the illusion of autonomy and the impossibility of life without a compelling obedience.
- Prophetic imagination names the impatience to which we are seduced and the inescapable waiting for gifts not yet received.

The circumstance generated by dominant imagination is an environment of complacency, self-sufficiency, anxiety, autonomy, and restlessness. That environment, however, is exposed and put at risk by the truth of YHWH's rule. Prophetic imagination thus counters dominant imagination as a practice that cannot give life because it fails at truth-telling.

4. The work of the prophetic is to trace the inescapable connections between personal pain and public systemic practice. Thus:

- Hosea moves from his own troubled marriage to the divorce and remarriage of YHWH with Israel (2:19-20).
- Amos can imagine a poor person with less than a pair of shoes and from that critiques an exploitative economy (8:6).
- Isaiah can imagine a national security state on endless Orange Alert, panicked by every little sign of threat, on which see also Leviticus 26:36 (30:17).
- Jeremiah can imagine an entry of military violence into one's bedroom and then ponders the results of self-destructive policy (4:20).
- Isaiah can imagine a mother forgetting a suckling child, while YHWH (with full breasts) will not forget Israel (49:15; see also 66:13).

The prophets consistently move from concrete experience but turn that concreteness into new truth that contradicts old truth held too long and too easily.

5. At the center of prophetic imagination is YHWH as a character and agent who is willing and capable of being the subject of active verbs. YHWH as agent is quite unlike the preferred gods who weakly assure but never enact any transformative verbs:

Our God is in the heavens;
    he does whatever he pleases.
Their idols are silver and gold,
    the work of human hands.

> They have mouths, but do not speak;
>   eyes, but do not see.
> They have ears, but do not hear;
>   noses, but do not smell.
> They have hands, but do not feel;
>   feet, but do not walk;
>   they make no sound in their throats. (Ps. 115:3-7)

And then the Psalm adds ominously, "Those who make them are like them; so are all who trust in them" (v. 8). It is this God in the heavens who can do whatever God wants, who occupies the commandments of Sinai, who delivered from Egypt, who refuses rivals and images, who models rest in an anxious world of production, and who prohibits acquisitiveness.

In the end, prophetic imagination is about deciding and redeciding. It is always about the either/or of life or death voiced in Deuteronomy (30:15-20). It is always redeciding for either the commoditization or available neighborliness of Israelite society in the eighth century BCE. It is always about deciding in the sixth century BCE about the pay-offs of empire of "that which does not satisfy" (Isa. 55:2) *or* an embrace of an alternative plan (vv. 6-9). In the twenty-first century, prophetic imagination concerns redeciding about images that generate attitude, conduct, and policy. In all such circumstance, it is redeciding about life or death.

Chapter 3

Loss Imagined as Divine Judgment

In their severe honesty, the prophets took the world as it was in front of them. But they saw that world very differently, because they saw it according to the God of the remembered imagination of the Torah tradition. And because they saw it differently, perforce, they spoke it differently. They could not do otherwise. Thus my thesis:

> Prophetic preaching is an effort to imagine the world as though YHWH, the creator of heaven and earth, the Father of our Lord Jesus Christ whom we Christians name as Father, Son, and Spirit, is a real character and decisive agent in the world.

I

The great prophets of the eighth and seventh centuries BCE—Amos, Hosea, Isaiah, Micah, Jeremiah, Zephaniah, the ones we name first as prophets—saw that the world of Israel-Judah (and the capital cities of Samaria and Jerusalem) was a society committed to long-term loss, grief, and, finally, termination. They perceived their society in this way because they recognized that their society was profoundly out of sync with the reality of YHWH, so out of sync that it could not endure. Not everyone, of course, perceived their world in this way. Those committed to the dominant reality of king and temple, not surprisingly, could not believe that such a loss was possible. They are the ones who said, in liturgical formulation, "Shalom, Shalom," when there was no shalom (Jer. 6:11; 8:14; Ezek. 13:10). But these prophets knew otherwise. What they knew otherwise evoked in them deep, daring, uncompromising poetry. What they offered was not more than poetry. But that poetry served well because it was an elusive articulation not easily co-opted or countered by the excessive certitude and high-handed dismissiveness of dominant imagination.

The Old Testament knows all about loss and grief.[1] It stands in the deep ancient Near Eastern culture of grief that it makes its own. At the most intimate level—that of personal, familial loss—Israel voices its grief. Father Jacob, when he finds the robe of his beloved son Joseph, makes the connection: "It is my son's robe!" (Gen. 37:33). And then we are told: "Then Jacob tore his garments, and put sackcloth on his loins, and mourned for his son many days. All his sons and all his daughters sought to comfort him; but he refused to be comforted, and said, 'No, I shall go down to Sheol to my son, mourning'" (vv. 34-35). He refused to be comforted! He wept all his days at his loss.

By the time of Jeremiah, the imagery has moved from father Jacob to mother Rachel. But it is the same grief:

> A voice is heard in Ramah,
>   lamentation and bitter weeping.
> Rachel is weeping for her children;
>   she refuses to be comforted for her children,
>   because they are no more. (Jer. 31:15)

Rachel could be comforted no more than Jacob. Only now it is not only their son Joseph who is lost. Now it is Israel lost, Jerusalem lost, all lost. And by the time of Matthew, when King Herod sought out all the baby boys in his sweep against imagined terrorists, the evangelist can quote:

> Then was fulfilled what had been spoken through the prophet Jeremiah:
>
> > "A voice was heard in Ramah,
> >   wailing and loud lamentation,
> > Rachel weeping for her children;
> >   she refused to be consoled, because they are no more."
> > (Matt 2:17-18)

Rachel weeps and Jacob weeps, all Jews weep. The church weeps. And God weeps. And before we finish, we come to Emil Fackenheim, who dares to say, "God Himself, as it were, weeps for His children. He weeps not for symbolic children in a symbolic exile, but for actual children in an actual exile. He weeps as would a flesh-and-blood father or mother. He weeps as Rachel does."[2] And then Fackenheim quotes the record from Nuremberg on Auschwitz: "When the extermination of the Jews in the gas chambers was at its height, orders were issued that the children were to be thrown straight into the crematorium furnaces, or into the pit near the crematorium, without being gassed first."[3] Jewish tears are endless for the loss.

And King David is like father Jacob. This man of immense power is a griever because he knows all about loss. He grieves the loss of his beloved Jonathan and his father Saul:

> Saul and Jonathan, beloved and lovely!
> > In life and in death they were not divided;
> they were swifter than eagles,
> > they were stronger than lions.
> O daughters of Israel, weep over Saul,
> > who clothed you with crimson, in luxury,
> > who put ornaments of gold on your apparel.
> How the mighty have fallen
> > in the midst of the battle!
> Jonathan lies slain upon your high places.
> > I am distressed for you, my brother Jonathan;
> greatly beloved were you to me;
> > your love to me was wonderful,
> > passing the love of women.
> How the mighty have fallen,
> > and the weapons of war perished! (2 Sam. 1:23-27)

There is a tone eloquent and formal about this loss, worthy of a king for a king. This is a king reduced to loss as he ponders what war does, so that potential victory turns sour on his lips.

When he had wept the poem, he was not finished. For he knew about his own son, the one he had conceived in lust with Bathsheba. He knew intuitively that his son was dead, as he acknowledged in resignation and helplessness: "While the child was alive, I fasted and wept; for I said, 'Who knows? The Lord may be gracious to me, and the child may live.' But now he is dead; why should I fast? Can I bring him back again? I shall go to him, but he will not return to me" (2 Sam. 12:22-23). No, he will not! The loss is deep and irreversible and so durable.

And even with Jonathan and the unnamed baby, David is not yet finished with his loss. Finally, there is his son with whom he has such a troubled relationship, for Absalom is his beautiful heir yet a renegade whom David's own men must kill. David is again in victory; but it is a thin victory. He knows of the death, and he cries: "O my son Absalom, my son, my son Absalom! Would I had died instead of you, O Absalom, my son, my son!" (2 Sam. 18:33).

And then, after a reprimand from Joab, yet again: "O my son, Absalom, O Absalom, my son, my son!" (2 Sam. 19:4).

What it must have cost David to humiliate himself and be scolded by his top general for his grief! What it must have cost the narrator, moreover, to find a way to chronicle this grief, for this king and this narrator are "acquainted with grief."

But of course Israel's tradition knows very well that grief is not confined to personal, familial loss, deep as that is. Israel finds words to move grief from the personal and the familial to the public and so Israel weeps the loss of the body politic even as parents stand over the beloved bodies of the children and weep. Thus Amos can sob over the house of Israel:

> Hear this word that I take up over you in lamentation, O house of
>   Israel:
> Fallen, no more to rise,
>   is maiden Israel;
> forsaken on her land,
>   with no one to raise her up. (Amos 5:1-2)

The poet can well ahead of time see Israel now fallen and forsaken, abandoned, with none to help. And Jeremiah can sharpen the imagery so that we can hardly bear the words about beleaguered Jerusalem:

> Consider, and call for the mourning women to come;
>   send for the skilled women to come;
> let them quickly raise a dirge over us,
>   so that our eyes may run down with tears,
>   and our eyelids flow with water.
> For a sound of wailing is heard from Zion:
>   "How we are ruined!
>   We are utterly shamed,
> because we have left the land,
>   because they have cast down our dwellings." (Jer. 9:17-19)

This is not only a death; it is a dying. It is a dying that lasts longer than any filmed death. It is a dying that has been under way for decades, even centuries; and no one noticed! This is a city that thought it was immune, beloved and chosen by God, and now death!

Eventually the anticipatory grief work of Amos and Jeremiah comes to full expression in the Book of Lamentations that sees now on the ground what the prophets had anticipated:[4]

> How lonely sits the city
>   that once was full of people!
> How like a widow she has become,
>   she that was great among the nations!
> She that was a princess among the provinces
>   has become a vassal.
> She weeps bitterly in the night,
>   with tears on her cheeks;
> among all her lovers
>   she has *no one to comfort her;*
> all her friends have dealt treacherously with her,
>   they have become her enemies. (Lam. 1:1-2)

The refrain, "none to comfort," sounds again and again in this poetry. It is an echo of Jacob and Rachel, for the body politic has no resources for well-being, and we refuse to be comforted:

> There is no one to uphold your cause,
>   no medicine for your wound,
>   no healing for you.
> All your lovers have forgotten you;
>   they care nothing for you . . . (Jer. 30:13-14a)

I linger so long over loss because I propose that prophetic preaching in our time and place fundamentally faces *the reality of loss* among us that dominant imagination could never, in its wildest imagination, imagine. That, I submit, is why 9/11 continues to move us so deeply. It is not about the loss of the buildings or even about some three thousand deaths, heavy as that continues to be. It is about breaking the code of invulnerability that we had so deeply trusted, now to discover that our best entitlements provide no protection. The shock among us is not unlike the shock in ancient Israel about Jerusalem. We—and they—never thought it could happen here—or there. We had chanted, "shalom, shalom" so long that we believed it.

There were always voices to the contrary who have witnessed before-hand to the fact that our society, like the ancient people of God, was out of sync with God. We have known about *the American Dilemma* of slavery and racism forever and its continuing violence until now.[5] Jeremiah Wright is only a recent version of those who noticed the distortion and anticipated the coming loss, and for noticing he was brutalized by the practitioners of the dominant narrative.

The wedge-point of 9/11 has, of course, gotten thicker. Now we watch while the economy is ditched by the greed of the big banks, the foolish-ness of subprime loans, and the avarice of deregulation. We have heard the gurgle from the Gulf with the oil spill as an icon of our technological self-destruction. With the collapse of well-being, we feel the deep anxiety among us signaled, for example, by the Tea Party movement. We notice the surge of ready violence all around us, all with the haunting sense that our old, unencumbered privilege is exhausted. The loss is everywhere palpable and the grief is deep indeed. And nobody but the poets can speak that loss. We arrive, like ancient Jerusalem, with a facade of well-being and a despairing anxiety beneath, because the world does not work for us anymore on our own terms, even if they are the terms of "chosenness." Eventually, we fall back on the artists and poets and preacher to speak sense when all of our technological futures have faded and no longer compel. And we want to say, "Does any-body care? Does anybody notice?"

> Is it nothing to you, all you who pass by?
>   Look and see
> if there is any sorrow like my sorrow,
>   which was brought upon me,
> which the LORD inflicted
>   on the day of his fierce anger. (Lam 1:12)

Does anybody know anything useful? Can anybody make a difference? We know down deep, moreover, that no "solution" will be found in the usual places. We also know, reluctantly, that we have to sit and wait and ponder and process and linger. And for that we require poets.

As I once reflected on this, the *New York Times* (September 19, 2000, pp. 1-13) featured, back-to-back, a) a news item about families who live in the great trash dumps of Cambalache, Venezuela, where they swarm around each new truck that dumps another load of garbage, in order to find food for the day; and b) a two-page ad for Armani jeans, "available only at Macy's" from Christine Ronaldo, featuring a shirtless virile wonder.[6] And we ask, does anybody notice? Does anybody care? Does anybody see the incongruity that must be unbearable to the Holy One of Israel?

II

Well, the poets notice. They always notice before anyone else. They bring to notice what remains elsewhere unnoticed. These poets, however, not only noticed, they noticed according to the propensity of Sinai; for them all of the memory and severity of Sinai seemed immediately pertinent to their present circumstance. When they revisited Sinai, they noticed the ominous "if" of Moses at the outset: "If you will obey my voice and keep my covenant, you shall be my treasured possession out of all the peoples. Indeed the whole earth is mine, but you shall be for me a priestly kingdom and a holy nation" (Exod. 19:5-6).[7] They noticed that the emancipatory initiatives of the God of the Exodus had been channeled into a relationship of mutual accountability that was codified in the book of Deuteronomy:

> Today you have obtained the LORD's agreement: to be your God;
> and for you to walk in his ways, to keep his statutes, his command-
> ments, and his ordinances, and to obey him. Today the Lord has
> obtained your agreement: to be his treasured people, as he promised
> you, and to keep his commandments; for him to set you high above
> all nations that he has made, in praise and in fame and in honor; and
> for you to be a people holy to the LORD your God, as he promised.
> (Deut. 26:17-19)

They pondered the agreement of Sinai and that to which Israel had agreed. They read in the scroll of Deuteronomy that everything depended upon justice to the *widow,* the *orphan,* and the *stranger.* In the interpretation of Moses, these three, together with *the poor,* became the test of obedience to the provisions of Sinai. They read in the Book of Leviticus that the practice of holiness was commanded: "You shall be holy, for I the LORD your God am holy" (Lev. 19:2). And the tradition lined out what that holiness meant for food and for sexuality and for farming and for every sphere of life. It turned out that the covenant of *justice and holiness* positions every part of life before the God of Sinai.

And then, as much as they could bear, they reflected on the tough sanctions given in both interpretive traditions. In Leviticus 26, they read about the big "if" of obedience that would guarantee security and prosperity and fruit-fulness (v. 3). And then they turned to the longer recital of warnings about disobedience that would yield defeat and drought and fear (v. 14). And perhaps even worse, they turned to Deuteronomy 28, which we will never hear in our public readings. The list of blessings is specific and quotidian:

> Blessed shall you be in the city, and blessed shall you be in the field.
> Blessed shall be the fruit of your womb, the fruit of your ground,
> and the fruit of your livestock, both the increase of your cattle and
> the issue of your flock.
> Blessed shall be your basket and your kneading bowl.
> Blessed shall you be when you come in, and blessed shall you be
> when you go out. (Deut. 28:3-6)

This recital of blessing is matched by curses for disobedience (vv. 15-19), followed by a long negative extrapolation (vv. 20-68).

The tradition of Sinai attested that the world is shaped in covenantal ways; YHWH is serious about the "agreements" and is the big "enforcer." They noticed that the negatives are much longer than the positives, as though the tradition was concerned that some would not get the seriousness of the requirement.

They must have treated these heavy texts gingerly, as though they were radioactive, like a hot potato that could burn your hand. Perhaps they recognized that the *tradition of justice* in Deuteronomy and the *tradition of holiness* in Leviticus are heavy-handed and coercive. Perhaps they judged that the traditions were naively supernaturalist and thought the warnings were a bit silly. Perhaps, like us, they were more than a little embarrassed about the simple-minded assumption that the world is so closely codified by covenant. Perhaps they wished they had never opened the scroll to these verses, and that they never knew about them. Perhaps they wished they could focus on better texts, like Abraham or David. But they found, like Victor Borge at the piano, that their hands and their eyes kept falling back on these dreadful teachings about the covenantal requirements of life with the uncompromising God who will not be mocked.

Well, I cannot think of any other way to acknowledge how difficult and awkward these texts are. I imagine that they put them aside. Such texts would never do in Jerusalem. But then, in the middle of the night, poems were given. Poems rose up at the interface between the lived reality of a narcoticized society and the old texts of agreement at Sinai. Poems were heard (and uttered) at the convergence of old imagination and present reality that required new imagination. These poets were haunted at night; they were at risk the next day when they said out loud what they had been given in the night. Indeed,

Jeremiah, for example, resisted the whole idea of being entrusted with these God-propelled poems (Jer. 1:6; 20:9). And like us, when his secretary, Baruch, was asked, "Tell us now, how did you write all these words? Was it at his dictation?" (Jer. 36:17). He answered only, "He dictated all these words to me, and I wrote them with ink on the scroll" (v. 18). Baruch did not say how Jeremiah got the poems. Likely he did not know. For who knows about poems and poets and being haunted and being at risk and offering utterance? Who knows, indeed?

III

Thus we have in the prophets these haunting poems given to haunted speakers. The prophets move back and forth between toxic social reality that only they seem to have noticed and the daily routine of social reality to which all gave casual assent and took for granted. The conclusion they draw, in their emancipated imagination, is that there is a profound, intransigent connection between old imagination from the Torah and present public reality. They are the ones who must connect the dots that dominant imagination does not want connected. Dominant imagination, moreover, does not believe that the dots can be connected, because we have long since banished the grounding agent of Sinai, banished either in Enlightenment rationality with a turn toward the subject or banished in benign religious friendliness of a therapeutic kind. It is certain that how they did the poetry is not the way we, in our contemporary prophetic preaching, might do the connecting.

But however we may be summoned to replicate their work, it is clear that loss is construed in their poetry as *judgment*. It is not *random loss* or *meaningless loss* or *accidental loss*. It is rather loss that has moral significance, even if we cringe from a moral "explanation" for what is lost among us. The world, so they say, is not a tale told by an idiot. It is rather a world governed by a faithful Lord who need not be lined out in supernaturalist simplicity, but who, in the end, will not be mocked. The poets voice the conviction that there is a connection between *choices* (attitudes, conduct, and policies) and *futures*. There is continuity and a coherence that cannot be voided. The task, based on long-term perspective, is to show how *choices produce futures*. There are blowback and unintended consequences that will not be evaded.[8] These poets seek out persuasive ways to voice the connections about which we do not want to hear. They foster rich rhetorical strategies for such utterance.

1. A primary strategy among these old poets is an appeal to "therefore," the all-purpose "ergo" that posits a linkage between what has gone before

and what comes after, a connectedness that dominant imagination believes, with its power and wisdom and wealth, it can overcome.[9] The examples of this usage are numerous in the prophets.

- In Hosea 4:3 the "therefore" stands between an indictment and a sentence. The indictment is recital of the commandments that have been violated:

    There is no faithfulness or loyalty,
        and no knowledge of God in the land.
    Swearing, lying, and murder,
        and stealing and adultery break out;
        bloodshed follows bloodshed. (vv. 1-2)

- The sentence concerns the dismantling of creation:

    Therefore the land mourns,
        and all who live in it languish;
    together with the wild animals
        and the birds of the air,
        even the fish of the sea are perishing. (v. 3)

The daring "therefore" makes a connection that depends upon a robust creation theology. The argument is that violation of the commandments of Sinai results in the collapse of creation. This is only an utterance. The poet eschews every scientific datum that might be used for the connection. But the connection is nevertheless the point. And now we, belatedly, dare to make the same connection about the environmental crisis with much more "data."[10] Hans Heinrich Schmid, in his definitive study, proposed that *Weltordnung* is *Gerechtigkeit,* "world order" is "righteousness"; and when that God-ordained righteousness, that life-giving energy and purpose is violated, world order is savaged.[11]

- In Amos 6:7, the prophet Amos utters a "therefore." Before it is a description, not unlike the Armani jeans of self-indulgent consumerism (vv. 4-6); after it, is the threat of displacement: "*Therefore* they shall now be the first to go into exile, and the revelry of the loungers shall pass away" (Amos 6:7). The coming consequence, says the poet, is displacement and deportation and the end of self-indulgence. But who would have thought of that connection? Who would conclude that too much wine or too many idle songs or too much veal could lead to deportation? Only a poet could make such an incommensurate connection.

• Micah 3:12 offers a "therefore" concerning Jerusalem. After it comes the threat that the city will be deserted and abandoned:

> *Therefore* because of you
>   Zion shall be plowed as a field;
> Jerusalem shall become a heap of ruins,
>   and the mountain of the house a wooded height. (Mic. 3:12)

This is the city of David where God dwells in the temple as "a very present help in trouble" (Ps. 46:1). The Songs of Zion had given assurance; such Psalms serve the dominant imagination.[12] Micah, however, proposes that his poem should veto such familiar liturgies of dominant imagination. And the ground for that judgment, before the "ergo," is a cryptic condemnation in which societal leaders are seen only as corrupt folk who then posture in all kinds of phony piety: "yet they lean upon the LORD and say, 'Surely the LORD is with us! No harm shall come upon us'" (Mic. 3:11). It is not difficult to critique self-serving corruption or phony piety. But these poets do much more than that. They discern the futures that such conduct will evoke; it is a future, on the far side of "therefore," that none thought possible in Jerusalem.

• In the long poem of Isaiah 5:8-25, the prophet in Jerusalem has recourse to four "therefores":

> *Therefore* my people go into exile without knowledge;
> their nobles are dying of hunger,
>   and their multitude is parched with thirst.
> *Therefore* Sheol has enlarged its appetite
>   and opened its mouth beyond measure;
> the nobility of Jerusalem and her multitude go down,
>   her throng and all who exult in her.
> . . . .
> *Therefore*, as the tongue of fire devours the stubble,
>   and as dry grass sinks down in the flame,
> so their root will become rotten,
>   and their blossom go up like dust;
> . . . .

> *Therefore* the anger of the LORD was kindled against his people,
>   and he stretched out his hand against them and struck them;
>   the mountains quaked,
> and the corpses were like refuse in the streets.
> (Isa. 5:13, 14, 24, 25)

The first of these again concerns deportation. The second, with more urgency, anticipates an opening abyss that will swallow the urban elites. The third is a fire upon those who have disregarded the Torah. And the fourth, with its first mention in this series of YHWH, is about divine anger.

We may notice that much of the talk of "therefore" in the prophets is without divine agency. Such agency is of course implied, but it is not stated. The prophetic rhetoric does not need to assert divine agency but can trace out the inescapable connection in a covenantally ordered world. On the other hand, they do not flinch from divine agency, for everything they have to say—about loss and about the future and about the connection between them—comes down to divine judgment; the world does not run on its own! To be sure, there is, here and there, talk of divine anger that is an embarrassment in our memo-writing world:

> For all this anger has not turned away,
>   and his hand is stretched out still. (v. 25)

But these words are not a memo. This is a poem. The poem utters the unutterable and thinks the unthinkable. We would not speak this way in the sober light of day. But this is the haunting of the night when we make compelling but illicit connections. The word of the night is that Jerusalem has created a situation so inimical to divine purpose that it cannot endure. The imagery is unbearable—earthquake, corpses—but the poets are the masters of hyperbole, which is put into the service of inscrutable, unaccommodating holiness.

IV

A second rhetorical strategy for transposing *loss* into *divine judgment*, that is, a second way of connecting the dots of lived reality, is by way of "woe oracles" that recur in the prophets. The term that introduces such oracles (*hoy*) is in NRSV variously translated as "ah," "ha," "oh," "alas." It is not, as popularly thought, a word of anger or threat. It is, rather, a word of sadness appropriate to death or other deep loss.[13] That is, it is an acknowledgment or anticipation of sadness over loss that is inescapable and unbearable, about which no one can do anything. It is most likely that the word arises in wisdom circles among those who noted, through long observation, the intransigent connection between cause and effect, between deed and consequence. Thus we might say, for example, "Woe to those who smoke; alas" (they will have throat cancer). Thus if one does a "foolish" thing long enough, the outcome of trouble is inevitable. The assumption of such wisdom observation is that the connection of *deed and consequence*, of *cause and effect*, is guaranteed by an order ordained by the creator, an orderliness that is essential to the prediction and replication of scientific experimentation.[14] Thus the connections are made on the surface of observation, but they are taken to be rooted in a connection that is below the surface and cannot be outflanked.

There are two extended series of such woe oracles in the prophets. In Isaiah 5:8-24, in which we have just seen four "therefores," there is a series of six "woes," albeit interrupted by other rhetorical maneuvers. In verses 20-23, we have a terse series of three such oracles:

> *Ah*, you who call evil good
>   and good evil,
> who put darkness for light
>   and light for darkness,
> who put bitter for sweet
>   and sweet for bitter!
> *Ah*, you who are wise in your own eyes,
>   and shrewd in your own sight!
> *Ah*, you who are heroes in drinking wine
>   and valiant at mixing drink,
> who acquit the guilty for a bribe,
>   and deprive the innocent of their rights!

Verse 20 warns of calling things by a wrong name, a practice among us of using euphemisms, so that the true character of the matter is disguised. Such a practice of euphemism was used most ominously by the National Socialists in Germany to disguise the death camps so that medical "experiments" were said to be a practice of medicine.[15] But the usage is present wherever the violence of war in the interest of the state is undertaken. In verse 21, the case concerns the arrogant, who think they know everything, "the Best and the Brightest." And in verse 22, the double warning is against those who get drunk and those who rule in court for a bribe. The parallel in the latter case suggests a loss of moral reference that evokes high-level corruption. These teachings offer a catalogue of behaviors that can only bring trouble. It is obvious, of course, that the teaching does not explain or trace out connections. The sayings are, however, based on ample practical evidence, so that the speaker knows that one cannot perform these acts with impunity. The deed itself will bring trouble.

A second series of such "woe" sayings is given in Habakkuk 2:6-19, which offers five "woes":

"*Alas* for you who heap up what is not your own!" (v. 6)

"*Alas* for you who get evil gain for your house,
     setting your nest on high to be safe from the reach of harm!"
     (v. 9)

"*Alas* for you who build a town by bloodshed
     and found a city on iniquity!" (v. 12)

"*Alas* for you who make your neighbors drink,
     pouring out your wrath until they are drunk,
     in order to gaze on their nakedness!" (v. 15)

Alas for you who way to the wood, "Wake up!"
     to silent stone, "Rouse yourself!" (v. 19)

The terse "woe" statement is supplemented in each case, but the primary claim is carried directly by the "woe." The dangerous actions that jeopardize society include avarice and coveting (vv. 6, 9) and exploitation (v. 12). The fourth case is curious (v. 15); it condemns drunkenness that leads to exposure. And the fifth case in verse 19 apparently concerns idolatry. Thus the recital is an inventory of distorted conduct that will skew neighborly relations and distort the life of the community. In its terseness the teaching does not explain. The function of the sayings is to observe and thereby to warn about the evocation of trouble by distorted behavior.

Finally, I note two such statements in Amos 6. In verse 1, the "alas" concerns complacency in Jerusalem. In verse 4, the term "woe" itself is, in translation, transferred from verse 1, for it is not in the Hebrew text. What follows in verses 4-6, however, is a characterization of extravagant self-indulgence that contains its own destructiveness. In this case the simple "woe" oracle has been drawn into other characteristic prophetic utterance, for in verse 7, as we have seen, there is an added "therefore" of deportation. The "therefore" itself is no normal part of the woe-oracle, for such a conclusion about coming punishment is not regularly made explicit, even though it is everywhere implied.

It becomes clear in the woe oracles, apart from the rhetorical supplements, that the trouble follows the conduct "automatically" and inevitably; there is no agent who initiates the consequence. There is no divine judgment and not even an appearance of God in such an utterance. The judgment comes because the world is ordered in such a way.

V

The two rhetorical strategies—the speech of judgment that pivots on the "therefore" and the woe oracles—are tightly disciplined, highly stylized maneuvers that intend to exhibit the human world in deep jeopardy. Beyond such severe rhetorical discipline, we may also notice that the prophets propose startling and affrontive imagery in order to penetrate the tight denial of dominant imagination.

Thus for example,

- Jeremiah can mix metaphors in a single poem so that he ridicules idolatry (2:27-28), references a bride who forgets her wedding dress (2:32), and anticipates military invasion that will cause humiliation (2:36). All of that in a single poem!
- Jeremiah can imagine one's sleep being interrupted by the intrusion of an enemy soldier that causes heart palpitations (2:19-21). The judgment of the oracle is not guilt but stupidity (v. 22): My people "do not know."
- Jeremiah can portray Jerusalem as a whore on the street waiting for a "hook-up":

> And you, O desolate one,
> what do you mean that you dress in crimson,
>> that you deck yourself with ornaments of gold,
>> That you enlarge your eyes with paint?
> In vain you beautify yourself.
>> Your lovers despise you;
>> they seek your life. (4:30)

But then the imagery shifts abruptly (v. 31). Now we have a woman left bereft in labor amid the military assault. The use of such sexual imagery is inescapably affrontive. But it is meant to be so! The poet wants to reach to the very bottom of emotional extremity to shake the obduracy of a people that refuses to notice.

When one considers these several strategies that appear in many guises in the prophets, two things become clear. First, the enormous rhetorical inventiveness shows that the poets use every device and strategy they can think of in order to *connect loss to the rule of God*. The *transformation of loss into divine judgment* is a move to show that the world is not autonomous but lives in a realm where the force of YHWH's will and purpose is definitive. Given that, however, one is struck by the infrequency with which YHWH directly intervenes as an agent of punishment. In many of the verses I have cited, there is little direct action by God. There are, rather, many ways to speak about loss as judgment that need not appeal to a crude intervention or a simplistic supernaturalism.

Second, one is struck as well by how rarely the prophets address specific social issues. They do not become advocates for particular issues, as is the case with much "liberal" "prophetic preaching." They aim beyond and beneath specific issues to the underlying governance of YHWH and the profound way in which Jerusalem must come to terms with that governance. Thus the penetration of the dominant imagination requires an address beyond issues to the governing assumptions of society that are rooted in autonomy and exposed as exploitative arrogance that is a non-starter in YHWH's world.

As we ponder loss transposed into divine judgment, we clearly have much to unlearn. First, the delicate, tricky way in which judgment is voiced requires an unlearning about "hell fire and damnation" in the name of God. Second, the characteristic refusal of the prophets to address specific issues requires an unlearning about liberal prophetic preaching that is often preoccupied with advocacy for specific issues. To be sure, the prophets cared intensely about neighborly justice and disciplined holiness, but their poetic imagination is seldom voiced toward specifics.

VI

I submit that the big issue for the prophets about loss is to insist that it is theologically meaningful. That is, they foster a narrative in which loss makes sense. It can be named and embraced and perhaps can invite a meaningful response. Life is not, in their testimony, random; it is governed and these poets, instructed by the remembered imagination of the Torah, know the name of the One who governs, even if that governance remains hidden and indirect. The prophets are, however, loath to reduce that agent of governance to a close formulation. They prefer that that governance be received in listening,

- as the fierce savagery of a lion;
- as the wistfulness of a wounded partner;
- as the freedom of a fearful storm;
- as a healing wind;
- as a balm that is given belatedly;
- as a lover who woos a second time;
- as a shepherd who seeks.

The prophets are committed to no single or normative set of images but offer images that witness to contradiction and that subvert every easy assumption.

Their insistence that things are connected is based on an appeal to the remembered covenant structure. The prophets ponder:

- What are the commandments that have been violated, even if they are commandments little recognized in dominant imagination?
- How are they broken when they are not hard rules but dimensions of a relationship that depends upon a committed fidelity?
- What would obedience require in which Israel has failed?
- What are the sanctions that reference covenantal expectation?

By appeal to the old tradition, the prophets insist that choices determine futures, that conduct matters decisively, and that things are morally connected. They make this insistence in the face of the temptation to believe that enough power, enough money, or enough shrewdness can outflank the connection. They insist that the connection is God-given and God-guaranteed, and no amount of posturing or pretence can grant immunity from the terms of covenant.

VII

Because the subject of "divine judgment" is exceedingly difficult, and because the topic is popularly caricatured in the language of Jonathan Edwards—how terrible to be "Sinners in the Hands of an Angry God"—it is worth a pause to consider critical reflection on the specific ways in which divine judgment in prophetic discourse may be understood. I will mention four recent scholarly reflections, each of which gives careful attention to the matter of divine judgment and each of which finds important restraint in the direct agency of YHWH who, in severity and anger, may punish Israel for its recalcitrance.

1. Klaus Koch has written the definitive article on the subject.[16] In retrospect, he has overstated his case; but his analysis is nonetheless the starting point for our consideration. Koch judges, on the basis of his reading of wisdom materials, prophetic oracles, and the Psalms, that there is very little "retribution" in the Old Testament that God directly and actively retaliates for covenantal violation. Instead of such direct "retribution," Koch finds that there is an "action-consequence" construal of covenantal order in which "Yahweh directs the exact consequences of an action back toward the person which corresponds to the prior action which that person started."[17]

Koch finds helpful the way in which seed eventuates in harvest: "It is understood that *the action is the seed*. A corresponding harvest comes out of what is planted. If the action is godless, then the consequent result is nothingness."[18] Or more colloquially, "What you sow you will reap," or even, "The chickens have come home to roost." Actions have built-in consequences, and YHWH guarantees that connection.[19] It does not surprise that we find this assumption in wisdom materials; but Koch has shown in compelling ways that much the same principle pervades "prophetic judgment." Divine judgment, in many cases, is the playing out of inescapable consequences of actions and decisions.

2. Patrick Miller, informed by Koch's work, has offered a rich analysis of prophetic texts of judgment.[20] His study takes full account of Koch's "built-in consequences" but suggests, further, that there is recurringly an exact correspondence in prophetic discourse between transgression and judgment, so that the quid pro quo provides that the offender receives in kind a consequence reflective of the affront. In this way the punishment is not arbitrary or random, but is closely linked to and informed by the affront. Thus for example, in Micah 3:10-12:

The affront: They

> build Zion with blood
> and Jerusalem with wrong!

The outcome:

> Zion will be plowed as a field;
> Jerusalem shall become a heap of ruins . . .

Miller opines that the reasoning is not unlike that of the "parity style" of international treaties and that the "talionic style" of quid pro quo is abundantly evident.[21] With Miller's "correspondence" as with Koch's "consequence," the active intervention of God as agent is quite subordinate. Things work out the way they do because the world is coherently ordered as God's creation.

3. In his study of the prophets, John Barton moves beyond Koch's analysis by proposing that something like "natural law" is operative in the prophets.[22] He works from specific texts, notably the Oracles against the Nations in Amos 1–2, and sees that the nations get back as punishment suffering that is commensurate with their international crimes. The affront need not be against Israel, but the blow-back is voiced when there is a brutal affront against any people. The God of Israel oversees all nations. The linkage of affront and outcome is not limited to Israel in these oracles.

> All the nations of the world are bound by certain moral laws and
> are accountable for their conduct; and Yahweh, the god who chose
> Israel as his special people, exercises a vigilant control over the way
> they act, punishing transgressions by causing war and so destroying
> sinful nations. Hence the fortunes of all nations are in Yahweh's con-
> trol, and this control is exercised according to ethical criteria.[23]

4. Terence Fretheim considers the same issue in his study of creation theology. He concludes:

> The moral order is fundamentally a matter of creation, built into
> the very infrastructure of God's cosmic design. That sins will have
> adverse consequences is fundamentally a matter of the way in which
> the world works; ill effects are intrinsically related to the deed. And
> so, it is a natural theological move for the prophet to follow the
> strong indictment and oracles of judgment (experienced and antici-
> pated) with a word about creation.[24]

For Fretheim the result of this connection is that one must be restrained in assuming that God actively and directly executes judgment against sinners. Fretheim places a major emphasis on the fact that there are historical agents who act out punishment for God in the public processes: "The people must be uprooted from the land for the sake of the land, but that end cannot be accomplished with a divine flick of the wrist."[25]

The prophets are not stupid or blindly supernaturalist. They have to persuade and make sense. They do not witness to a deus ex machina, but they pay attention to the lived processes whereby the plots of historical drama are variously brought to conclusion.

These several studies testify against any simplistic notion of divine judgment. Of course we must fully accept the deep claim that "God judges." But clearly the matter is complex and the prophets are careful and persuasive in finding ways to mediate the claim of divine judgment in ways that take account of the real world that has irreducible moral shape.

VIII

The matter of divine judgment, in our discussion, is a subset of the matter of loss: Jerusalem is a community in loss. It finally experienced the loss that the prophets had long anticipated and seen beforehand. For that reason, we must pay attention to the way in which divine sternness is qualified by divine grief. Thus Fretheim attends to such grief on God's part over the coming trouble for the city:

> We are helped in thinking about it by the other dimension of God's response to the situation, namely, grief. The personal, emotional, and repetitious language shows how much this is a genuine loss for God. Given the divine commitment to people and land and the centuries-long relationship with them, God cannot (!) respond indifferently. God is truly caught up in what has happened here and mourns the loss.[26]

Behind Fretheim, as he himself notes, is the moving judgment of Abraham Heschel about the loss on God's part:

> Israel's distress was more than a human tragedy. With Israel's distress came the affliction of God, His displacement, His homelessness in the land, in the world. And the prophet's prayer, "O save us," involved not only the fate of a people. It involved the fate of God in relation to the people. For Israel's desertion was not merely an injury to man; it was an insult to God. . . . The Lord who had dwelt in the midst of Israel was abandoning His dwelling place. But should Israel cease to be His home, then God, we might say, would be without a home in the world. He would not have left His people altogether, but he would be among them like a stranger, like a wayfarer, withholding His power to save. It is as if there were an inner wrestling in God.[27]

Thus God is not offered in this poetry as one who foams in righteous indignation. Rather God experiences and voices the sadness that anticipates what is to come that cannot be averted. It is as though God were helpless before the inexorable law of "the Medes and the Persians," so that God will not (cannot?) actively intervene to disrupt the steady flow from deed to consequence.[28] As a result, YHWH watches and grieves over YHWH's own people concerning its inescapable trouble to come. Evidence of such divine suffering over the coming suffering of God's people is clear in a variety of texts:

> O that my head were a spring of water,
> and my eyes a fountain of tears,
> so that I might weep day and night
> for the slain of my poor people! (Jer. 9:1)

> Take up weeping and wailing for the mountains,
> and a lamentation for the pastures of the wilderness,
> because they are laid waste so that no one passes through,
> and the lowing of cattle is not heard;
> both the birds of the air and the animals
> have fled and are gone. (Jer. 9:10; see 3:19-21; 12:7)

Thus divine judgment is not a contractual matter. It is a covenantal, relational transaction in which much is at stake for God in the implementation of consequences. It is no wonder that the poets must move toward images of *husband and wife* and *parent and child* in order to catch the complexity and pain of wrath-grief that causes divine judgment to be an act of felt loss. When judgment is taken at face value without reference to loss, the matter is misperceived as though God had no stake in the transaction. In the end, as we shall see, it is that stake, that deeply felt stake that eventually pushes beyond judgment toward restored historical possibility.

IX

We may consider two texts that together, in tension, exhibit the rich complexity of divine judgment in prophetic tradition. In Amos 7:1-9, we are given access to the triangle of violated covenant, the triangle of YHWH, Israel, and the prophet. In order to catch the pathos, we must see that the three transactions in the text are of a piece:

(a) In verses 1-3, there is the coming of locust, surely a "natural" phenomenon, but understood as a covenant curse. The initial description makes nothing of the dimension of punishment. It is simply an agricultural threat, enough of a threat to evoke a prophetic petition. The petition for forgiveness suggests the locust are seen by the prophet as punishment. The petition of the prophet reflects pathos-filled anguish, sure to evoke divine response:

> O LORD God, forgive, I beg you!
> How can Jacob stand? He is so small! (v. 2)

"Jacob" is vulnerable and helpless; YHWH "relents," moved by the petition and the suffering of Israel.

(b) In verses 4-6, a parallel transaction is performed. This time it is a "judgment of fire" in which the prophetic petition is sharper: "Halt!" There is no doubt that YHWH is seen as the agent of the fire. But it is the vulnerability of Israel ("so small") that moves YHWH yet again to "relent." c) In the third vision of a "plumb line," there is no petition and so no "relenting." Now there is only the settled divine verdict introduced by "behold." Judgment is coming and YHWH will be the perpetrator.

What interests us is the movement through the three episodes. It is the same God who *relents* and then *relents*, and then *declares judgment*. God is moved by prophetic petition, and is moved by prophetic petition, and then is not open any more to petition. The sequence suggests a divine process in which God weighs the vulnerability and need of Israel over against the provocation against YHWH that has been lined out in previous oracles by Amos. It is as though the actions of Israel had set in motion punishing consequences that can no longer be delayed. The oracle attests to the limit and exhaustion but also the reality of divine forbearance.

In Hosea 11:1-9, the drama goes differently. The tension between Israel and YHWH is more fully framed. Whereas Amos 7:1-9 begins abruptly, Hosea 11:1-9 begins with a retrospect on YHWH's generous fidelity toward Israel (vv. 1-4). But the move to judgment in verse 5 is abrupt. The judgment is submission of Israel to the perennial brutal threats, Egypt and Assyria. The imperial vehicle of suffering, of course, is "the sword" that moves decisively and brutally against "their schemes," that is, their autonomous defiance of YHWH's intent. The judgment is imperial, with no direct action taken by YHWH.

At the end of verses 5-7, "they call." They no doubt call and petition as did Amos. But there is no divine answer, just as there was no divine answer, finally, in Amos 7:9. Without divine response, Israel is left with the out-working of the sword that their own actions have evoked. By the end of verse 7, we are in a situation very like that of Amos 7.

Except of course, the oracle continues. YHWH relents and exhibits compassion. YHWH now refuses to enact "my fierce anger," for YHWH now embraces and acknowledges and exhibits YHWH's own radical otherness ("not mortal"). We are not told why this now, but surely it relates to the courage of the poet.

I have juxtaposed these two prophetic oracles in Amos 7 and Hosea 11 as a study in the complexity of divine judgment. The sequence in Amos 7:1-9 moves from *relenting forgiveness* to *hard-nosed judgment*. In Hosea 11, the movement is in the other direction, from *judgment* to *compassion*. In both cases the trouble is evoked by sin. Thus Amos asks forgiveness for Israel, and Hosea mentions "schemes." In both cases the punishment is articulated. The resolutions of the two transactions, however, exhibit different dramatic performances, from compassion to judgment or from judgment to compassion. The contrast is not because Amos is a poet of justice and Hosea is a prophet of love, as we often say. For there is enough of judgment in Hosea. The contrast exhibits the rhetorical maneuverability the poets were free to exercise. In both cases, we are given glimpses into the poet's imagination of the internal processing of the God of the covenant toward wayward Israel. In the Amos oracle, God reaches the end of forbearance. In the Hosea oracle, God moves abruptly, in self-assessment, to compassion. In both cases, the oracle of divine intentionality is linked to but is distant from the working out of social judgment whether implemented or stayed. What we have is poetic utterance that relates to and stands apart from historical reality. "Prophetic imagination," in these two instances, is poetry that invites the listener to consider the plight of God in the drama of fidelity and infidelity. A flat rendering of divine judgment misses the thickness of the poetry, for the poetry exhibits the divine struggle that Fretheim characterizes as "tremendous loss" for God.[28] In missing that thickness, moreover, we likely at the same time to miss the thickness of the human process that transpires among those who listen to the rendering of God's internal life. The offer of *God's internal life*, as the prophets risk it, may give us access to *our own unresolved internal life*.

X

It remains to comment on our contemporary task of prophetic preaching. I have proposed that the task, now as then, has to do with loss and insists that loss, deep and broad as it is, can be situated morally in covenant context.

The prophetic tradition has a full inventory of losses, and we in our time and place know that inventory:

- The loss of a guaranteed economy and thus job prospects;
- The loss of confidence in government, since no one now knows how to cope;
- The loss of understanding between generations, exacerbated by emerging technologies;
- The loss of communication skills in a rapidly changing world;
- The loss of old moralities;
- The loss of US dominance in a world of wars we cannot win;
- The loss of our conviction about exceptionalism that was, we thought, immune to violence;
- The loss of a center that no longer holds;
- The loss of old certitudes;
- The loss of a viable "natural" environment;
- The loss of a world peopled only by "our kind."

That wide and deep loss generates immense anxiety that is largely amorphous and unacknowledged. It is an anxiety that eventuates in anger and fear, that invites nostalgia, that tempts to privatism, and that seeks scapegoats.

Prophetic preaching knows more than the inventory of loss. It knows something that connects the dots of shattered experience into a meaningful narrative account of reality. Such awareness is not propelled by either righteous indignation or zealous advocacy. It trusts the tradition and is not immobilized by questions about its "historicity." It is not enthralled by an ideology of right or left. It has for that reason, at its best, a kind of freedom for truth-telling that does not coerce.

That freedom issues in poetic imagination that lets the world be seen as a world where God's ordered intentionality prevails.[29]

- It practices candor and calls things by their right names;
- It anticipates losses yet to come, without being in the prediction business;
- It instructs, without a didactic tone, so that listeners can know enough about the covenant to see the connection between normative commandments and inescapable sanctions.
- It appeals to a rich inventory of images and metaphors, while adding fresh ones that give access to reality beneath the radar of dominant imagination.

Thus we get, just in Hosea for example:

> Maggots and rot (5:12),
> Lion and young lion (5:14),
> Spring rain (6:3),
> Morning dew and clouds (6:40),
> Heated oven and a cake not turned (7:4-8),
> Silly dove (7:11),
> Vulture (8:1),
> Whirlwind (8:7).

The preacher says, as did the ancients:

> Just imagine!
> Just imagine loss!
> Just imagine loss in which something is at stake for God!
> Just imagine loss over which God grieves!
> Just imagine loss and name it and dwell in it;
> Dwell in it amid other dwellers in that loss.
> Dwell in it in the presence of God who is mix of severity, grief,
>   and relenting compassion.

Kenneth Doka has written about "Disenfranchised Grief" by which he means grief unowned, unacknowledged, unshared, and unappreicated.[30] The dominant narrative disenfranchises grief because it cannot afford to be honest. And grief disenfranchised leads, as we know, to denial and, finally, to violence. But prophetic preaching permits acknowledged, anticipated grief, and gives franchise to grief felt and embraced. When grief is owned, as we know, it turns to energy, resolve, and new possibility.

The risks of transposing loss into divine judgment are at least three:

- When the dots are connected, it will require naming the defining sins among us of environmental abuse, neighborly disregard, long-term racism, self-indulgent consumerism, all the staples from those ancient truthtellers translated into our time and place. Who would have thought, except people with this "therefore," that these distortions could bring all the maladies that now beset us? Connecting the dots is hazardous in a society that does not want to know.
- When the poet connect the dots in a way that reflects the order guaranteed by the creator, that poet risks dismissal, and we run

the risk of foolish freedom in a society that has driven God from the public square.

- Finally, prophetic preaching collides with US exceptionalism, just as the old prophets collided with Jerusalem exceptionalism. That, I judge, is the most immediate and palpable risk of dot connection. For that process makes clear that the dots are visible even in this blessed commonwealth that cannot bear such a thought.

Two conclusions:

1. Alfred Tennyson, in his poem *In Memoriam* (1850), wrote words that we know from the hymn, "Strong Son of God," which in recent time has been reduced to "Incarnate God":

> Our little systems have their day,
> They have their day and cease to be.
> They are but fleeting certainties,
> And You, O Christ, are more than they.[31]

Imagine, in ancient Jerusalem or in the twenty-first century United States, that "our little systems have their day and cease to be." There is, for our little systems, loss and judgment; our little systems—political, economic, moral, and ecclesial—are at best fleeting certitudes without staying power. And God is more than any of them or all of them. The move in the poem of Tennyson, and in all prophetic poems, is the move from our "little systems" to the God who is "more than they."

2. In the stunning recital of Hebrews 11, the text has it: "All of these died in faith without having received the promises, but from a distance they saw and greeted them. They confessed that they were strangers and foreigners on the earth . . ." (11:13-14). And in Hebrews 13:14: "For here we have no lasting city, but we are looking for the city that is to come." The present city will not last. We imagine its loss. In our next discussion, we will consider the ways in which the prophets imagine the city that is yet to come.

4

A Lingering Place
of Relinquishment

THE WORLD OF JERUSALEM, as the prophets find it, was on its way to loss.
They imagined that the loss was linked to YHWH as divine punishment.
They imagined, outside the box of establishment excuses and explanations,
that the destruction of the city and the forced departure from the city were
because of Israel's long-term recalcitrance against the Sinai covenant. They
imagined differently, as though YHWH were inevitably front and center in
their discernment of the city. Thus my thesis:

> Prophetic preaching is an effort to imagine the world as though
> YHWH, the creator of heaven and earth, the Father of our Lord
> Jesus Christ whom we name as Father, Son, and Spirit, is a real char-
> acter and the defining agent in the world.

There is no doubt that the prophetic theme is divine judgment, though, as we
have seen, the pending punishment is not voiced simply as supernatural intrusion but as the inescapable outworking of the deeds and policies of Jerusalem
that evoked devastating consequences.

I

If the prophetic theme had been simply divine judgment, it might have been
resolved, in their imagination, simply as guilt, punishment, and perhaps

71

repentance. Or it could have been rendered simply as anger toward God and rejection of God that evoked a like response from God who then had anger toward Israel and rejected Israel. It is, clear, however, that divine judgment is in fact a subset of the overriding reality of loss. Loss, as we all know, admits of no quick resolution. It lingers; and we linger in it. It lingers through the long nights with unrelenting force. And when it does, one has no option but to live with it and hopefully to live through it. And because loss is the over-whelming reality and divine judgment is a subset of prophetic imagination that seeks to make sense out of loss, I want in this presentation to explore the awareness that divine anger, rejection, and alienation are decisively qualified, in the prophetic horizon, by the working of empathy. For loss per se does not of itself indicate anger. It is marked by anger from God only if the loss is known to be punishment. But if loss is more elemental than judgment, then I propose that empathy is even more elemental than anger. The issue is impor-tant because much of our notion of prophetic preaching revolves around divine anger and consequently righteous indignation. Here I observe that we have, in such a caricature, missed the prophetic point that divine judgment is shot through with divine pathos, a theme first celebrated in contemporary interpretation by Abraham Heschel.[1]

And if "empathy" witnesses to the claim that YHWH is deeply moved, troubled, and staggered by Israel's loss, then the pathos of God, the pas-sionate feeling of God, eventuates in empathy and in sympathy, in solidar-ity that in biblical terminology comes as compassion (passion—"to suffer," com—"with," compassion—"to suffer with.") Thus YHWH is imagined as standing alongside Israel in its loss, as though YHWH were helpless to avert the loss, as though the loss were as acutely felt by YHWH as it was felt by Israel. The move of pathos from the lived experience of Israel to the des-ignated experience of YHWH is indeed an act of imagination. Unless we embrace that act of imagination, however, loss becomes unvexed punishment on the part of YHWH. Contrary to that, the prophetic texts witness that YHWH is profoundly vexed by Israel's loss that must, perforce, be enacted in Jerusalem.

In this discussion. I will consider the process of Israel's pathos over loss, and then I will reflect on YHWH's pathos over that loss. I will trace these twin dimensions of pathos to the bottom and watch the move to recovery from pathos. Both Israel and YHWH will, in the prophetic drama, move beyond pathos. But neither will move quickly or easily or clearly beyond, for loss leaves its mark. In this connection, I am reminded of the shrewd quip of the great New York senator, Patrick Moynihan, when he reflected on the assassination of John F. Kennedy and witnessed the ongoing loss for

Jacqueline and her entourage of which he was a part. He said of the Kennedy grief, perhaps of all the United States caught up in that death and its deep, incalculable loss: "We shall laugh again, but we shall never be young again." Israel, after its loss, will laugh again. But Israel is like a parent who has lost a child; such a parent will never be young again. And YHWH? YHWH has lost hugely in the crisis of the Old Testament. YHWH has lost the city and the people and the temple and the covenant; YHWH will never be young again. But YHWH will laugh. It will be an Easter laugh. It will, however, be a scarred laugh, never free of Friday, never recovered from the loss of the Son or the loss of city and temple, because the loss endures for all parties. The prophets could anticipate that loss that was sure to come upon Israel.

It was not just anticipation however; the loss was unmistakable in their observation. They had data for their judgment. And from that data the prophets imagined toward YHWH. They imagined that YHWH felt the same loss, wept the same tears, grieved the same grief, forfeited the same youth, and refused for now to laugh. Such prophetic poetry need not be loud or confrontational or self-assured. It is tinged with pathos, with empathy, with sympathy, with compassion. None of that overrides the reality of judgment. But it gives tone and nuance and depth to the lived reality. Poetic Israel, that is, Israel troped in this poetry, is proud and defiant and recalcitrant. But poetic Israel is also stupid, so that it forfeited futures for itself without knowing that it did so:

> The ox knows its owner,
>   and the donkey its master's crib;
> but Israel does not know,
>   my people do not understand. (Isa. 1:3)

> Even the stork in the heavens
>   knows its times;
> and the turtledove, swallow, and crane
>   observe the time of their coming;
> but my people do not know the ordinance of the Lord. (Jer. 8:7)

The God of this people is filled with indignation but also with pathos because of futures chosen by Israel that nobody one would deliberately choose. The unwitting quality of those choices makes the loss no less real and deep; it does, however, position the loss as more complex than mere anger. During the long night, there is a waiting to see if Israel can laugh again. Or if YHWH can laugh again.

II

Israel of course has a long liturgical, pastoral history of grief work in its many lament Psalms.[2] But those laments are especially mobilized around the crisis of the fall of Jerusalem, its king, its temple, and its status as the chosen of YHWH. Two Psalms line out the grief of that loss.

Psalm 74 described for YHWH in careful detail the way in which the Jerusalem temple has been sacked and abused by the enemy:

> Your foes have roared within your holy place;
> > they set up their emblems there.
> At the upper entrance
> > they hacked the wooden trellis with axes.
> And then, with hatchets and hammers,
> > They smashed all its carved work.
> They set your sanctuary on fire;
> > they desecrated the dwelling place of your name,
> bringing it to the ground.
> They said to themselves, "We will utterly subdue them";
> > they burned all the meeting places of God in the land.
> We do not see our emblems;
> > there is no longer any prophet,
> > and there is no one among us who knows how long. (vv. 4-9)

The complaint turns to wonderment about YHWH's lack of engaged attentiveness:

> How long, O God, is the foe to scoff?
> > Is the enemy to revile your name forever?
> Why do you hold back your hand;
> > why do you keep your hand in your bosom? (vv. 10-11)

The Psalm culminates with a strong series of imperatives that do not doubt YHWH's capacity to redress the situation. Appeal is made directly to the covenant with the expectation that YHWH will subdue the enemy and restore the well-being of the community:

> Remember this, O Lord, how the enemy scoffs,
> > and an impious people reviles your name.
> Do not deliver the soul of your dove to the wild animals;

> Do not forget the life of your poor forever.
> Have regard for *your covenant*,
>> for the dark places of the land are full of the haunts of violence.
> Do not let the downtrodden be put to shame;
>> let the poor and needy praise your name. (vv. 18-21)

In this Psalm, there is no thought that the destruction of the temple is divine punishment, nor is there any thought that YHWH has perpetrated this unbearable loss.

> In Psalm 74, the concept of YHWH's wrath (v. 1) is combined with the motif of the absence of God (v. 3) which is used to express the thought that since YHWH has abandoned his people, Israel's enemies can ravage the land. This divine absence is mysterious (v. 10f.) and can consequently not be remedied by help of a confession of sin (see also Psalms 60; 80; 89).[3]

It is thus inferred that YHWH has been negligent and has permitted the enemy to invade. This Psalm assumes that the appeal to the covenant is still proper and that YHWH is obligated to act for Israel as covenant partner.

In Psalm 79, the situation is somewhat altered. Again the bulk of the prayer is a characterization of the humiliating suffering of loss:

> O God, the nations have come into your inheritance;
>> they have defiled your holy temple;
>> they have laid Jerusalem in ruins.
> They have given the bodies of your servants
>> to the birds of the air for food,
>> the flesh of your faithful to the wild animals of the earth.
> They have poured out their blood like water
>> all around Jerusalem,
>> and there was no one to bury them.
> We have become a taunt to our neighbors,
>> mocked and derided by those around us.
> How long, O Lord? Will you be angry forever?
>> Will your jealous wrath burn like fire?
> Pour out your anger on the nations
>> that do not know you,
> and on the kingdoms
>> that do not call on your name. (vv. 1-6)

Again there is "How long?" But here there is reference to divine anger and wrath that is matched in verse 8 by an acknowledgment of iniquity on the part of Israel:

> Do not remember against us the iniquities of our ancestors;
>> let your compassion come speedily to meet us,
>> for we are brought very low. (v. 8)

In this latter Psalm there surfaces the thought that the loss is divine punishment. Even so, however, this is not a major accent in the Psalm. There is, to be sure, the voicing of remorse and a bid for forgiveness. Nonetheless Israel's loss goes directly to petition that assumes it can appeal for YHWH's help, that it is entitled to do so, and that YHWH has some obligation to respond to the petition of Israel. First there is a prayer that YHWH's anger be transferred from Israel to the enemy:

> Pour out your anger on the nations
>> that do not know you,
> and on the kingdoms
>> that do not call on your name. (v. 6)

And then there is a series of imperative petitions:

> Help us, O God of our salvation,
>> for the glory of your name;
> deliver us, and forgive our sins,
>> for your name's sake.
> . . . .
> Let the groans of the prisoners come before you;
>> according to your great power preserve those doomed to die.
> Return seven fold into the bosom of our neighbors
>> the taunts with which they taunted you, O Lord! (vv. 9, 11-12)

The major accent is still on the enemy and the conviction that faithful YHWH will counter the threat of the enemy. Compared to Psalm 74, however, we are on the way to a more focused prophetic accent on divine judgment.

In the prophetic tradition there is an anticipation of loss that will evoke wailing and crying grief. This is not in the nature of a prediction; it is simply a recognition that violations of covenant bring with them covenantal sanctions. Or alternatively, it is a conviction that certain kinds of deeds bring inescapable consequences. In Amos 5:16-17, the poet imagines grief at loss that is connected to YHWH's "passing through" as one who will destroy:

> Therefore thus says the LORD, the God of hosts, the Lord:
> In all the squares there shall be wailing;
>   and in all the streets they shall say, "Alas! Alas!"
> They shall call the farmers to mourning,
>   and those skilled in lamentation, to wailing;
> in all the vineyards there shall be wailing,
>   for I will pass through the midst of you,
>   says the LORD.

And in Amos 8:1-2, there is a word play and a meditation on "the end" that will come upon Israel:

> "The end has come upon my people Israel;
>   I will never again pass them by."

The response to "the end" will be wailing over death:

> "The songs of the temple shall become wailings in that day,"
>   says the Lord GOD;
> "the dead bodies shall be many,
>   cast out in every place. Be silent!" (v. 3)

Worth notice is the double use of the term "pass" (*'avar*) in both texts; in 5:17, it is divine "pass through" that is ominous. In 8:3 it is divine "pass through" that might have protected them. In both uses, the trouble is acutely YHWH-framed that evokes immense grief.

In Micah 1:8-16, we are offered a poetic lament in which the prophet lines out grief over Jerusalem:

> For this I will lament and wail;
>   I will go barefoot and naked;
> I will make lamentation like the jackals,
>   and mourning like the ostriches.
> For her wound is incurable.
>   It has come to Judah;
> it has reached to the gate of my people,
>   to Jerusalem. (vv. 8-9)

There is no doubt that the subject of the lament is Jerusalem. And the reference to an "incurable wound" indicates the depth of the misery that will come on the city. The lament is echoed in 2:4. The poet traces the avarice of the wicked that will evoke evil and that in turn will evoke bitter wailing. The wailing, so the poet anticipates, will be lined out in a lament that seems to be YHWH's one lament for "my people." But now it is clearly the lament of the community:

> On that day they shall take up a taunt song against you,
>   and wail with bitter lamentation,
> and say, "We are utterly ruined;
>   The Lord alters the inheritance of my people;
> how he removes it from me!
>   Among our captors he parcels out our fields."

> While the poet connects the coming loss to YHWH's "devising
> evil" (v. 3), the lament itself in verse 4 makes no acknowledgment
> of guilt. Nor does it implicate YHWH in the act, as though it were
> divine punishment. This is a much more elemental act of loss, of
> being "utterly ruined." (See Isaiah 3:24 on the concreteness of being
> "utterly ruined.")

The prophets invite Israel to grieve. The prophetic anticipatory figuring of loss is an attempt to break the denial and to bring the community to active grieving that is commensurate with its coming circumstance. For the most part, divine punishment seems to be implied, but it is not often stated in the lament. The accent is not on YHWH's involvement but upon the brute fact of loss. Such a lament from the people is quoted in Jeremiah 8:20:

> The harvest is past, the summer is ended,
>   and we are not saved.

The lament of the people in this case is taken up by the prophet in a longer lament by YHWH. In chapter 9, Jeremiah has YHWH call for the women who are recognized in the community as competent grievers:

> Thus says the Lord of hosts:
> Consider, and call for the mourning women to come;
>   send for the skilled women to come;
> let them quickly raise a dirge over us,

> so that our eyes may run down with tears,
>   and our eyelids flow with water.
> For a sound of wailing is heard from Zion:
>   "How we are ruined!
>   We are utterly shamed,
> because we have left the land,
>   because they have cast down our dwellings." (Jer. 9:17-19)

The quoted lament in verse 19 is closely parallel to the one we have found in Micah 2:4. In Jeremiah 9:20-22, the stakes are raised in the rhetoric. Again there is an appeal to the women to perform a dirge. But the actual lament in verse 21 is even more extreme:

> "Death has come up into our windows,
>   it has entered our palaces,
> to cut off the children from the streets
>   and the young men from the squares."

Death is now an active agent who breaks into the palatial homes often thought to be safe and impenetrable. The consequence of this active agent, death, is a heap of corpses:

> Thus says the LORD:
> "Human corpses shall fall
>   like dung in the open field,
> like sheaves behind the reaper,
>   and no one shall gather them." (v. 22)

In none of this is YHWH mentioned, and in none of it is Israel said to be guilty. It is all loss!

We are able to find such statements of grief even in the lyrical poetry of Isaiah, where they are quoted only to be refuted. In Isaiah 40:27, the poet quotes a lament that must have been much used, perhaps liturgically:

> "My way is hidden from the LORD,
>   and my right is disregarded by my God."

The loss has led Israel to the conclusion that YHWH was no longer faithful to Jerusalem. It is not said that YHWH has punished, only that YHWH is absent and negligent. It is divine disregard that has permitted the enemy to do the destruction of the city. In Isaiah 50:2, the poet has YHWH refute the accusing lament. Thus the lament is not stated as such but is cited only to be answered:

> Is my hand shortened that it cannot redeem?
> Or have I no power to deliver?

YHWH, since the exodus, has worked with "a strong hand and an outstretched arm" on behalf of Israel. When YHWH's hand is shortened, YHWH can no longer perform such saving work. Thus the conclusion has been drawn in Israel, one that is here refuted, that the loss has come because YHWH is powerless to prevent it. The same lament is implied in Isaiah 59:1 wherein YHWH makes a claim to the contrary:

> See, the LORD's hand is not too short to save,
>   nor his ear too dull to hear.

And in Isaiah 49:14, the lament of Jerusalem is quoted:

> But Zion said, "The LORD has forsaken me,
>   my Lord has forgotten me."

Most likely this is a quoted lament from Lamentations 5:20, where the same word pair is used. The accusation is not that YHWH has performed the loss but has, by negligence, permitted the loss to occur. In the end, it is a charge of faithlessness against YHWH.

In all of these texts, we are able to see that grief and punishment hover around the edges of the rhetoric. But they are not the main point. The main point is loss that raises questions about YHWH's fidelity or capacity. These questions, however, are not primary, even in prophetic utterance. What is primary is raw, concrete, fully described loss, now uttered in the context of faith in YHWH.

This honest articulation of loss, without excessive theological adornment or interpretation, is quite clearly central to prophetic faith. It occurs to me that prophetic preaching will do well to present word and gesture for the processing of loss. The role of covenantal YHWH and therefore the categories of covenantal failure and covenantal punishment are at the edge in the poetry. But they are not central. We can see Israel, in these poems, lingering in the grief and voicing it boldly. That function of prophetic preaching is important, because in a society of buoyant denial as ours is, there is no venue for public grief. It is required, in the dominant narrative, to rush past loss to confident "recovery" according to a tight ideology of success. But loss requires lingering. Thus Israel knows that "weeping may linger for the night" (Ps. 30:5):

> I am weary with my moaning;
>   every night I flood my bed with tears;
>   I drench my couch with my weeping.
> My eyes waste away because of grief;
>   they grow weak because of all my foes. (Ps. 6:6-7)

> My tears have been my food
>   day and night,
> while people say to me continually,
>   "Where is your God?" (Ps. 42:3)

> In the day of my trouble I seek the Lord;
>   in the night my hand is stretched out without wearying;
>   my soul refuses to be comforted. (Ps. 77:2)

The night is that long season of vulnerability when the ideological assurances and surveillance of dominant culture no longer protect us and we descend to the full reality of our bodies. The "winners" may loudly proclaim that "It is morning in America." But those in loss know better. They wait for the morning; they know very well that the dawn cannot be rushed or restored ahead of time. The prophets were in tune with such pastoral reality and dared to go, in their utterances, into the raw places of loss that had been declared "off limits" by dominant imagination.

I propose that the elemental circumstance of prophetic preaching in the United States is the deeply felt, seldom acknowledged reality of loss. We may have no doubt, as the ancient prophets in Jerusalem had no doubt, that loss was a consequence of failed fidelity. In the depth of the night, however, theological reprimand is not what is needed. What is required, rather, is the honest voicing of the reality of loss. In our society we are now losing the "old world" we have been taught to imagine as our achievement, a world of security and prosperity and entitlement. And now that world is departing from us—economically, politically, culturally. Sadness is co-opted as anger. There are times for the prophets to connect the dots of loss and failed covenant, of choices made that produce unbearable futures. In the night, however, the dots do not need to be and cannot be connected. It is enough tell the truth of bitterness:

We are utterly ruined. (Mic. 2:4)
How we are ruined! (Jer. 9:19)
My right is disregarded by my God. (Isa. 40:27)

All true! There are reasons for the ruin. But they will wait. For now, in the night, the circumstance requires a God who is no longer young. The God who waits is, for the span of the night, helpless before the intransigent choices that Jerusalem has made.

III

Eventually, at long last, after waiting in the null, there comes the light of dawn when "the long nightmare is over." Israel comes to know, and to trust, that "joy comes in the morning" (Ps. 30:5). Weeping does end; grief is exhausted; loss reaches its bottom where there are no more words or tears. YHWH, in Israel's loss, had been perceived as incompetent or uncaring or impotent. As I have suggested, however, the laments of Israel have been taken up in the lyric of Isaiah. YHWH is moved to answer after the long night with a response that transforms. As is characteristic in Israel's laments in the book of Psalms, there is divine response. That fresh utterance of YHWH opens new possibility. Thus in Isaiah, we may see as examples three cases in which quoted lament is now answered decisively by YHWH's new resolve:

- The lament in Isaiah 40:27 is:

   "My way is hidden from the LORD,
      And my right is disregarded by my God."

The divine answer concerns new empowering engagement:

   The LORD is the everlasting God,
      the Creator of the ends of the earth.
   He does not faint or grow weary;
      His understanding is unsearchable.
   He gives power to the faint,
      and strengthens the powerless.
   Even youths will faint and be weary,
      and the young will fall exhausted;
   but those who wait on the LORD shall renew their strength,

> they shall mount up on wings like eagles,
> they shall run and not be weary,
>> they shall walk and not faint. (vv. 28-31)

- In Isaiah 50:2, the implied lament is:

> Is my hand shortened, that it cannot redeem?
>> Or have I no power to deliver?

The divine response is:

> By my rebuke I dry up the sea,
>> I make the rivers a desert;
> their fish stink for lack of water,
>> and die of thirst.
> I clothe the heavens with blackness,
> and make sackcloth their covering. (vv. 2-3)

- In Isaiah 49:14, the quoted lament is:

> "The Lord has forsaken me,
>> my Lord has forgotten me."

The divine response is:

> Can a woman forget her nursing child,
>> or show no compassion for the child of her womb?
> Even these may forget,
>> yet I will not forget you.
> See, I have inscribed you on the palm of my hands;
>> your walls are continually before me. (vv. 15-16)

The divine response, in lyrical force, each time overpowers the lament. We do not know, in each case, if the answer prevailed. Surely it prevailed among those who were ready to relinquish what had been lost, who had completed their grief over loss. There is no doubt, in the lyric of Isaiah, that the divine response gives new futures. For some who heard, it may not yet have been time. Some no doubt lingered longer in the night. And in our own prophetic preaching, there are folk who linger and do not hear, because the grief is not yet completed. But the poet has YHWH acknowledge that there has been divine silence and reticence long enough:

> For a long time I have held my peace,
>> I have kept still and restrained myself;
> now I will cry out like a woman in labor,
>> I will gasp and pant. (42:14)

YHWH brings energy and resolve and emotive power to birth a newness:

> I will lay waste mountains and hills,
>> and dry up all their herbage;
> I will turn the rivers into islands,
>> and dry up the pools.
> I will lead the blind
>> by a road they do not know,
> by paths they have not known
>> I will guide them.
> I will turn the darkness before them into light,
>> the rough places into level ground.
> These are the things I will do,
>> and I will not forsake them. (vv. 15-16)

The corner is turned! Now there is no more divine judgment. That has been satisfied (see 40:1-2). YHWH is ready with newness. It is, however, a newness only given when Israel has relinquished what has been treasured and lost. Only in the work of relinquishment is newness given. No doubt now in our society, there is much that has been treasured among us that will be relinquished. But until it is relinquished, there will be no newness. This process, voiced by the prophet, is a process of letting go that creates space for new gifts.

Our preoccupation here is with Israel's loss. But when the prophets imagine with reference to YHWH, they turn matters away from Israel's loss to YHWH's own internal life. Joy does come in the morning. But we may pause to consider how it has been for YHWH and what has triggered in YHWH a readiness to speak and act anew in the moment of loss.

IV

The prophetic-pastoral task is to provide a script of imagination whereby folk can linger in our loss and then be done with the loss in order to move on. But because this prophetic script of imagination is preoccupied with

YHWH, who is the primary character and agent—in prophetic horizon—of loss and newness, I turn now from the human, Israelite process of grief and hope to the same process of grief and hope in the internal life of YHWH. Because they are poets, the prophets dare to claim access to the internal life of YHWH that is complex, conflicted, and unresolved. This effort on their part of course puts the prophets in profound tension with "normative theologies" that thrive on unambiguous certitude. "Normative theologies," like the Deuteronomist, allow for no playfulness in their dictums of certitude. But the prophets, in their daring utterances, are not finally Deuteronomists, and they do not traffic in certitude. They traffic rather in elusive imagination that keeps opening life and reality out to another dimension.

The prophets, so rooted in the remembered imagination of the Torah (and of Deuteronomy), found ground for such elusive playfulness, for example, in the self-declaration of YHWH in Exodus 34:6-7.[4] After the crisis of broken covenant with the golden calf in Exodus 32, YHWH, together with Moses, had to renegotiate and redecide about the future of the covenant. YHWH declared about YHWH's self, in 34:6-7, that YHWH is a God of abiding fidelity:

"The Lord, the Lord,
a God merciful and gracious,
slow to anger,
and abounding in steadfast love and faithfulness,
keeping steadfast love for the thousandth generation,
forgiving iniquity and transgression and sin,"

But YHWH also had to add:

"yet by no means clearing the guilty,
but visiting the iniquity of the parents on the children
and the children's children,
to the third and fourth generation."

This elemental declaration about fidelity and "visiting iniquity" discloses YHWH's unsettled state and YHWH's room for maneuverability. In this most elemental tradition, YHWH is disclosed, imagined in poetic form, to be an agent of elusive complexity. And then, belatedly, in the tough days of loss and displacement, the prophets dare to play upon that elusive complexity. They know in strange ways that what is going on in the hidden life of YHWH is more decisive than what appears to be going on in the world.

They claim, astonishingly, to disclose what is hidden about YHWH's internal life. It is of course hazardous to map out in thematic fashion that which
is given to us as elusive poetry. I suggest, nonetheless, that we can trace, in
a rough way, the movement of self-regard in the character YHWH that is
deeply rooted in the self-declaration of Exodus 34.

It is surely true that YHWH takes affront at Israel's recalcitrance. In
important ways, a prophetic perspective on the life of Israel before YHWH
is a continual reiteration of the narrative of the golden calf. To that crisis
YHWH responded with angry indignation: "I have seen this people, how
stiff-necked they are. Now let me alone, so that my wrath may burn hot
against them and may consume them; and of you [Moses] I will make a great
nation" (32:9-10). According to the prophets, YHWH's wrath continues to
flourish over the centuries. The prophetic speech of judgment (that I have
traced with a "therefore" and a "woe") witnesses to this God who will not
be mocked. The prophetic speech of judgment, with full emotive force, gives
voice to YHWH's uncompromising self-regard. Those who violate that divine
self-regard are bound to receive from YHWH flowing wrath that consumes.
I will not develop that theme, as the data is well known. On the one hand,
that speech of judgment is disciplined and symmetrical, as Patrick Miller has
shown; it actualizes a quid pro quo from an even-handed judge who gives
what people deserve.[5] On the other hand, however, there is an emotive dimension of YHWH's indignation that moves beyond the symmetry of quid pro
quo to dangerous, out-of-control anger. The extreme case of such divine over-
flow is that of Ezekiel wherein YHWH is an affronted husband who voices
violent destructiveness against wife Israel:

> Because your lust was poured out and your nakedness uncovered in
> your whoring with your lovers, and because of all your abominable
> idols, and because of the blood of your children that you gave to
> them, therefore, I will gather all your lovers, with whom you took
> pleasure, all those you loved and all those you hated; I will gather
> them against you from all around, and will uncover your naked-
> ness to them, so that they may see all your nakedness. I will judge
> you as women who commit adultery and shed blood are judged,
> and bring blood upon you in wrath and jealously. I will deliver
> you into their hands, and they shall throw down your platform
> and break down your lofty places; they shall strip you of your
> clothes and take your beautiful objects and leave you naked and
> bare. They shall bring up a mob against you, and they shall stone
> you and cut you to pieces with their sword. They shall burn your

houses and execute judgments on you in the sight of many women; I will stop you from playing the whore, and you shall also make no more payments. So I will satisfy my fury on you, and my jealousy shall turn away from you; I will be calm, and will be angry no longer. (Ezek. 16:36-42)

There is no way that such an emotive threat can be contained in the rationality of covenantal judiciousness. The prophet is driven to the imagery of husband-wife in order that the infidelity of Israel can be faced in its most extreme form, and in order that YHWH's passion can receive full sway. Such divine emotional "out-of-control" is not, however, very far removed from YHWH's response to the golden calf in Exodus 32:9-10. YHWH is known, in the tradition, to be a jealous God who acts on that jealousy.

V

It is clear however, at the same time, that YHWH is not single-minded about the condition of Israel as it suffered both the consequence of symmetrical covenantal sanctions and as it received the emotional reaction of YHWH. That double articulation of *formal sanctions* and *personal assault* results, for Israel, in immense loss (as I have traced it), loss of king, temple, city, and loss of confidence in the covenantal fidelity of YHWH. The startling realization of the prophets is that YHWH, in the midst of emotive reaction, also suffered the loss. The destruction of Jerusalem and the displacement of the people amounted to a huge loss for YHWH. YHWH lost YHWH's residence (the temple) and YHWH's anointed agent (the king); YHWH also lost a covenant partner on whom YHWH had lavished much long-term generous attention. Because of that deep loss for YHWH, the poets find that YHWH is driven to deep grief over the loss. It was clear to the prophet that YHWH the lingered in grief over the loss. This point should not be overstated in the tradition, and prophet must have reckoned it to be a subordinate note alongside divine indignation. But it is there, and it has been largely disregarded among us.

The remarkable articulation by the prophets, seen most clearly by Abraham Heschel, is that YHWH's anger and indignation are interrupted and qualified by YHWH's pathos-filled sense of loss. There is, to be sure, never a hint that YHWH's anger is inappropriate or that YHWH's indignation is not merited. And as long as the relationship is understood in symmetrical, contractual terms, that is the end of the story. But of course biblical faith, and the God of the Bible, do not and are not capable of staying within such categories.

YHWH as agent and as character breaks out of those categories into emotive commitments.[6] It is likely the latter that is more interesting and more important for contemporary preaching, for it is that divine emotive commitment that opens a way for Israel as it does for YHWH.

Divine indignation is a given, and well deserved. It is, however, the move beyond indignation that belongs properly to prophetic faith and prophetic preaching. Here I will line out a series of texts that show this remarkable move beyond indignation that characterizes the God of the Bible. It will be evident that I am finally dependent upon Heschel. It is my hope, nonetheless, that this inventory of divine grief will make a correction to our usual thinking about the prophetic. The sum of my argument in this regard is that YHWH, in response to YHWH's own loss, is driven to grief. That grief, moreover, becomes the fulcrum for newness for Israel and for YHWH.

1. Surely the lead example for entry into the internal life of YHWH is the poem of Hosea 11:1-9 that traces out the emotional journey of YHWH in relation to Israel. The poem begins in a reminiscence about the earlier time of shared well-being (vv. 1-4). It moves, as the poet will, into harsh divine rejection of Israel (vv. 5-7). In the depth of the coming crisis, it is anticipated, Israel will turn to "the Most High." But the God to whom appeal is made does not answer, having withdrawn from Israel in anger (v. 7). That much of the poem ends in judgment and displacement. We are, in conventional prophetic indignation, completely unprepared for verse 8 that follows. The poet does not tell us what happened to YHWH between verse 7 and verse 8, but it was clearly some flash of self-consciousness on YHWH's part. After the pause when YHWH speaks again, the tone is radically altered. Now, in a self-reflective moment, YHWH examines YHWH's own actions and motivations:

> How can I give you up, Ephraim?
>   How can I hand you over, O Israel?
> How can I make you like Admah?
>   How can I treat you like Zeboiim?

Gerald Jansen has nicely suggested that the questions are not rhetorical but in fact they are serious probes for self-understanding.[7] YHWH resolves to forego wrath and to commit to compassion that exhibits YHWH's best self. It is this compassion (*krm*) that differentiates God from "man" (v. 9). Everything important in this sequence is hidden from us between verses 7 and 8. Perhaps Hosea does not know what has happened, except that he may know from his own experience of suffering love. In any case, he does not tell us but is content to let that intense moment of divine transformation remain concealed. He only tells us of the consequence of that transformation: YHWH has moved through *anger* to *anguish* over the proposed judgment against Israel, and from anguish on to *new resolve* to be fully and credibly and responsibly and freely God (El).

2. Isaiah 22:1-8. The poem tracks the abdication of public leaders (vv. 1-3) and the consequent "day of YHWH" that exposes Jerusalem to coming military violence (vv. 5-8). Verses 1-3, 5-8 voice a standard prophetic judgment. Except that in the midst of it, verse 4 is an odd disruption:

> Look away from me
>   let me weep bitter tears;
> do not try to comfort me
>   for the destruction of my beloved people.

The speaker is clearly YHWH who refers to "my people," who are being destroyed. YHWH is reduced to tears, even though destruction of the city is merited. In the company of Jacob (Gen. 37:35) and Rachel (Jer. 31:15), YHWH refuses to be comforted. It may be that that moment of divine grief is not yet poignant enough to disrupt the anticipated judgment of Israel. Indeed, it sounds here as though the God of Israel is helpless before the inexorable work of consequences for Israel's choices, not unlike the intransigent "law of the Medes and the Persian." YHWH can only weep in sadness for the destruction that must be enacted. But the counter-theme of divine sadness begins to build that will become increasingly important, in prophetic rhetoric, in the face of the judgment to come.

3. That counter theme of divine sadness and grief takes on fresh force in the grief of Jeremiah 8:18-9:3. Four times in the poem, YHWH refers to "my poor people" (8:18, 21, 22; 9:1). In fact the Hebrew is "my daughter people," but the NRSV rendering evokes the pathos that belongs to the poem. As we have seen, the poetry quotes the people's lament in 8:20, as well as the people's fearful wonderment in 8:19:

> "Is the LORD not in Zion?
>   Is her King not in her?"

The folk utterances, however, are now situated in the longer lament of YHWH who is driven to grief over the coming fate of Jerusalem.

The poem continues in 9:1-3 with a deft traditioning move. It is commonly noted that 9:1-2 is a direct allusion to Psalm 55:6-8:

And I say, "O that I had wings like a dove!
   I would fly away and be at rest;
Truly I would flee far away;
   I would lodge in the wilderness;
I would hurry to find a shelter for myself
   from the raging wind and tempest."

Only now the yearning to escape the turmoil is placed on YHWH's lips. It is YHWH who cannot bear the affliction of Jerusalem and the suffering that is to come upon the city. YHWH is reduced to tears as YHWH ponders the coming trouble on YHWH's beloved "daughter" who is "not saved." In this text, there is no judgment but only pained, wistful rumination on what is unbearable for this caring parental figure.

4. The ante is upped, as Kazo Kitamore has seen, in Jeremiah 31:20, wherein YHWH asks questions reminiscent of those in Hosea 11:8:[8]

Is Ephraim my dear son?
   Is he the child I delight in?

The two questions require a "yes" in response. Yes, this is YHWH's dear son. Yes, this is the child in whom YHWH delights. Yes, YHWH remembers "Ephraim" and cannot disregard him. Yes, even in the depth of anger and consequent destruction and displacement, YHWH remembers.

As so often in the prophets, as we have seen, the poem moves to a "therefore." But now, it is a very different "therefore." Now it is a result drawn not from Israel's conduct, as is usually the case, but from YHWH's own critical self-reflection. The "therefore" is followed by two statements of self-recognition. First, YHWH observes what happens to YHWH as YHWH ponders the loss of Israel:

I am deeply moved for him . . .

The remembering of Israel whom YHWH had tried to forget causes agitation for YHWH. But second, YHWH makes a new resolve that is expressed with the intensity of an infinitive absolute:

I will surely have mercy on him . . .

YHWH's resolve for the future does not derive from the petition of Israel or even the circumstance of Israel. It derives from YHWH's recognition of

YHWH's own propensity. That propensity, moreover, contradicts the torrent of judgment that has been pronounced. It is that contradiction of justified divine anger that becomes the basis for the future. YHWH, from now on, will attend to the enactment of compassion.[9]

5. The larger poetic unit of Jeremiah 30:12-17 maps out the same remarkable movement in YHWH's propensity toward Israel.[10] In verses 12-15, with an allusion to the hopeless illness of Israel in 8:21-22, the accent is on the incurable sickness of Israel:

> Your hurt is incurable,
>   your wound is grievous.
> . . . .
>   Your pain is incurable.

That terminal illness, moreover, is the inescapable consequence of sin:

> . . . I have dealt you the blow of an enemy,
>   the punishment of a merciless foe,
> because your guilt is great,
>   because your sins are so numerous.
> . . . .
> Because your guilt is great,
>   because your sins are so numerous,
>   I have done these things to you. (vv. 14-15)

These lines are characteristic prophetic indignation. And they lead, as we have come to expect, to the "therefore" of verse 16.

Except that this "therefore" is no ordinary "therefore." It does not, as we have been led to anticipate, lead to a severe sanction of judgment. Rather it introduces a dramatic inversion in the relationship. Now YHWH will be Israel's advocate and defender who will "restore health to you." In a remarkable about face, the "incurable hurt" of verse 12 will be transformed to health. The God who has savaged Israel with a helpless diagnosis in verse 17 now reverses field and becomes the healer.

The poem voices a radical reversal in divine intentionality. YHWH occupies the poem and performs the reversal. We are not told how that reversal happens, though the change clearly has occurred between verses 15 and 16. When we notice the repeated phrasing in verses 14 and 17, we are given a clue about the basis for the change. In verse 14, YHWH declared of Israel's allies, "they care nothing for you." And then, in verse 17, in a sort of reprise,

YHWH overhears Israel's detractors asserting that "no one cares for her." The first declaration is on the lips of YHWH and refers to the former allies who no longer care about Israel. But the second, on the lips of the erstwhile allies, declares that not even YHWH cares. The second line echoes the first; only now it involves YHWH, along with the allies, in the abandonment of Israel. It is as though YHWH recognizes, in that moment of accusation by the nations, how the decision to destroy Jerusalem sounds to those who watch.

It is as though YHWH now takes seriously the warning and advice that Moses offered in Exodus 32:12 and Numbers 14:13-16:

> Why should the Egyptians say, "It was with evil intent that he brought them out to kill them in the mountains, and to consume them from the face of the earth"?
>
> . . . .
>
> But Moses said to the LORD, "Then the Egyptians will hear of it . . . and they will tell the inhabitants of this land. They have heard that you, O LORD, are in the midst of this people. . . . Now if you kill this people all at one time, then the nations who have heard about you will say, 'It is because the LORD was not able to bring this people into the land he swore to them that he has slaughtered them in the wilderness.'"

It is as though YHWH must now act for YHWH's self-regard to refute the conclusion drawn by hostile observers. More than that, it is as though in this moment of readiness, YHWH discovered a depth of commitment to Israel that YHWH had not, until now, acknowledged. We might wish to penetrate deeper into the hidden zone between verses 15 and 16, but we are given enough. We are able to see the way in which YHWH is "converted" from anger to healing resolve. We are permitted to see the way in which the "incurable hurt" of Israel impinges upon YHWH in order to compel a new resolve of restoration:

> Therefore all who devour you shall be devoured,
>   and all your foes, everyone of them, shall go into captivity;
> those who plunder you shall be plundered,
>   and all who prey on you I will make a prey.
> For I will restore health to you,
>   and your wounds I will heal,
>   says the LORD,
> because they have called you an outcast:
>   "It is Zion; no one cares for her!" (Jer. 30:16-17)

6. Isaiah 42:14-16. Now, belatedly in exile, it is as though YHWH has finally been moved to new self-assertion on behalf of Israel. It is as though YHWH has watched mutely while Babylon has done its destructive on Israel, Babylon acting out of its own arrogant self-regard (see 47:7-10). For whatever reason, the poet knows that YHWH can no longer keep silent while Israel is abused:

> For a long time I have held my peace,
>   I have kept still and restrained myself;
> now I will cry out like a woman in labor,
>   I will gasp and pant. (Isa. 42:14)

The divine silence is broken, not by a formal memo or an edict of new policy. It is broken by a cry and a gasp and a pant. It is broken by labor pains or "like" labor pains. It is broken with extreme emotional force, a force evoked by the suffering of Israel and by YHWH's solidarity in that suffering.

And now follows an inventory of divine self-resolve in first person verbs:

> I will lay waste,
> I will dry up,
> I will turn,
> I will lead,
> I will guide,
> I will turn.

This is the resolve of the great creator God who will transform the world in which Israel lives. The trigger for all that follows in the new resolve is YHWH's inability to endure any longer in silence the suffering of Israel. It is that divine inability to stay with the punishment that becomes the ground of new forceful resolve and therefore new historical possibility.

7. Isaiah 49:15-18. In response to Israel's complaint (already cited), YHWH is portrayed as a mother of a nursing child. No, rather YHWH is portrayed as better than a nursing mother. In its displacement, Israel had concluded that YHWH had forgotten and forsaken (Lam. 5:20). If YHWH had been a nursing mother, she might have forgotten, as it does happen, says the poet. But YHWH is not a nursing mother, at least not a conventional one. Thus YHWH's self-announcement contradicts Israel's conclusion. The poem does not tell us or even speculate, in the midst of YHWH's abidingness, how the displacement of Israel could have happened or lasted as long as it did. The accent is on the claim that the displacement of Israel did not disrupt YHWH's

remembering of or fidelity toward Israel. Indeed, YHWH might have forgotten Israel, except Israel's name is inscribed for YHWH to see and to remember (v. 15).

That data-defying affirmation about YHWH's remembering of Israel leads to compassion. As Phyllis Trible has noted, the play of words for "womb" and "compassion" witness to a mother-like passion and compassion for Israel into the future.[11] The practical evidence for such a conclusion, says the poet, is the historical act of gathering to homecoming. Thus the poem makes no compromise with the seeming abandonment of Israel by YHWH but moves on to the assured future.

8. Isaiah 62:1 is an echo of 42:14. Again YHWH acknowledges having kept silent. But now the silence is broken. Now YHWH will be active and engaged on behalf of Israel. The purpose of YHWH's new resolve is the vindication of Jerusalem and its restoration to well-being and prosperity:

> They shall be called, "The Holy People,
> The Redeemed of the LORD";
> And you shall be called, "Sought Out,
> A City not Forsaken." (v. 12)

Israel is now fully reestablished and Jerusalem is fully restored. The city now defiantly refuses any notion of "forsaken." The parallel to "not forsaken" is "sought out." Of special interest is the fact that the verb "sought out" (drš) is twice used in Jeremiah 30:14, 17, rendered as "cared for." It is as though this poem intentionally answers the poetry of Jeremiah 30. The one abandoned is now "married" (v. 4; see 54:4-6).

This rich array of texts leads to a remarkable sum. Taken together they do not deny divine anger, indignation, and punishment. They do however, indicate that YHWH's restless awareness that such anger and indignation cannot be the final word; YHWH continues to be haunted by and preoccupied with Israel, even in the midst of and after judgment. The poets thus trope the internal life of YHWH who moves in and through the judgment of Israel.

First, YHWH is portrayed as reduced to deep grief about the loss of Jerusalem and the suffering of Israel:

> O that my head were a spring of water,
> and my eyes a fountain of tears,
> so that I might weep day and night
> for the slain of my poor people! (Jer. 9:1)

> Look away from me,
>   let me weep bitter tears;
> do not try to comfort me
>   for the destruction of my beloved people. (Isa. 22:4)

Second, YHWH breaks the silence to which YHWH had been reduced, whether by anger or sadness, or a combination of the two. YHWH is compelled to Israel in its need and so must intervene:

> For a long time I have held my peace,
>   I have kept still and restrained myself;
> now I will cry out like a woman in labor,
>   I will gasp and pant. (Isa. 42:14)

> For Zion's sake I will not keep silent,
>   and for Jerusalem's sake I will not rest . . . (Isa. 62:1)

Third, the new resolve of YHWH, evoked at the nadir of loss, is a fresh commitment to compassion that wells up from YHWH's own intention and that receives historical actualization in restoration:

> I will not execute my fierce anger;
>   I will not again destroy Ephraim;
> for I am God and no mortal,
>   the Holy One in your midst,
>   and I will not come in wrath. (Hos. 11:9)

> Is Ephraim my dear son?
>   Is he the child I delight in?
> As often as I speak against him,
>   I still remember him.
> Therefore I am deeply moved for him;
>   I will surely have mercy on him,
>   says the LORD. (Jer. 31:20)

> Even these may forget,
>   yet I will not forget you.
> See, I have inscribed you on the palms of my hands;
>   Your walls are continually before me. (Isa. 49:15-16)

And of course, the "caring" and "healing" of Jeremiah 30:17 constitutes an expression of that same compassion.

Thus YHWH is indeed beset by anger and a propensity to punish. That is a serious contention of the prophets who insist that the historical process has a moral shape given by YHWH the creator that cannot be outflanked. That much we knew.

But prophetic preaching that focuses just there, as is conventional in "prophetic preaching," misses the deeper intention of these poets. In the very midst of such indignant self-regard, YHWH of these poets falls into grief and lingers there. Thus the terse New Testament report that "Jesus wept" (John 11:35) is fully congruent with the God he serves. Jesus wept in a death scene over Lazarus. But Jesus has more weeping to do, also over Jerusalem that kills the prophets and that would come to a very sorry end (Luke 19:41-44; see 13:31-35). The God of Israel has been weeping over Jerusalem forever. That same God weeps over the savage judgment that comes in the historical process. But that same weeping, it is attested, becomes ground for new possibility.

VI

I have suggested that the human process of lingering over loss (sometimes experienced as judgment) and moving beyond loss to new possibility is a practice that preoccupies prophetic preaching. In a society either beset by denial (that refuses to acknowledge loss) or committed to despair (that settles in to abiding loss), the prophetic task is the voicing of *the process of loss* that moves through grief to possibility. That process is a bold contradiction of these twin societal temptations.

That *human process of loss–grief–new possibility*, I propose, has a forceful counterpoint in the same plot for divine life in Israel's prophetic poetry. The God of Israel *lingers over loss*, *grieves over loss*, and finds *impetus for new possibility* in the loss when it is fully embraced.

Now this may sound, dear reader, like a peculiar notion of prophetic preaching. It is, however, fully faithful to the text and, I have no doubt, appropriate in a society of reductionism that cannot entertain the human process of loss with its divine counter-point, and could not imagine a divine process through grief to newness. The task of prophetic preaching then, is to break the immobilizing grip of such reductionism, to subvert the simplistic explanatory logic of dominant imagination, and to permit access to the thickness of processed grief wherein hides newness waiting to be enacted.

Israel vigorously voices its sense of being abandoned and forsaken and forgotten, the sense we all know in the depth of loss. In some texts, moreover, YHWH with equal vigor denies that there has been forgetting, forsaking, or abandoning on YHWH's part. But Israel, in its candor, is not fully or easily persuaded by such divine denial. Israel is pressed to protest and complaint, a necessary protest to give full voice to loss.

And then, as though the protest finally breaks through YHWH's resistant denial of infidelity, YHWH can also issue a new address and new assurance. Such a word of assurance may follow the imagery of a barren woman who now will have many children (Isa. 54:1-3) or the image of a widow disgraced but now reengaged (54:4-6). To that barren woman and that disgraced widow (both stand-ins for Israel), YHWH now, in a remarkable moment of self-acknowledgment, dares to concede:

> For a brief moment I abandoned you,
> . . . .
> In overflowing wrath for a moment
> I hid my face from you . . . (Isa. 54:7a, 8a)

The abandonment and hiding have been for a moment. In Israel's experience that "moment" is a long era of exile. That is how it is in our loss. Every occasion of loss is experienced as "forever."

But the poet will finally not allow YHWH's concession to stand on its own. The confession of YHWH is followed immediately, in both verses, by a second line:

> . . . but with great compassion I will gather you.
> . . . .
> . . . but with everlasting love I will have compassion on you,
> says the LORD, your Redeemer. (Isa. 54:7b, 8b)

The two lines in each of these two verses provide an epitome of the process. The poet will require YHWH to admit the abandonment; but the poet will also allow YHWH to speak another word that moves beyond the alienation to new well-being grounded in fidelity. Neither line is permitted to cancel out the other. Both are true, in sequence. We are not told how YHWH, or the poet, was able to move, in each verse, from the first line to the second line. Between the two lines in each verse, there is scarcely a pause, enough for a comma. That comma of loss and abandonment, however, is defining for many with whom we preach.

But the poem moves along. It hurries along to the second line in each verse. And in each case, there is an offer of compassion, of solidarity and empathetic companionship. Nothing is denied from the first lines. Everything is conceded. In this instance, either the poet or YHWH judges that we have lingered at the comma long enough. And now the new word is "compassion" as basis for new possibility.

As though to override the loss and move beyond it, the poem in verses 9-10 changes the subject and moves to a different image, the ancient, remembered flood of Noah. Every serious loss—even those given as judgment—is experienced as a flood in which we are helplessly inundated. Prophetic preaching must voice the flood of loss.

And then comes the promise of "never again":

> Just as I swore that the waters of Noah
>   would *never again* go over the earth,
> so I have sworn that I will not be angry with you
>   and will not rebuke you. (Isa. 54:9)

> I will remember my covenant that is between me and you and every
> living creature of all flesh; and the waters shall *never again* become a
> flood to destroy all flesh. (Gen. 9:15)

The "never again" of hope arises for Israel exactly in the face of abandonment. But the "never again" arises for YHWH as well, right in the face of abandonment. It issues for YHWH in steadfast love, a covenant of peace, and yet again, compassion:

> For the mountain may depart
>   and the hills be removed,
> but my *steadfast love* shall not depart from you,
>   and my *covenant of peace* shall not be removed,
>   says the LORD, who has *compassion* on you. (Isa. 54:10)

The promise is given by YHWH who "compassions you!" The verb is an intensive *pi'el* participle. Compassion is being done in the very utterance, done with all the intensity of the *pi'el* stem of the verb. Thus the move out of loss (as judgment) and grief is through the uttered assurance that we are being "compassioned." Imagine being a prophetic preacher who has that to say about loss as judgment. There is a lingering in loss for God and for Israel. That lingering, however, is not a final end. Because the silence is broken. Joy

does come in the morning (Ps. 30:5). It cannot be hurried; but it also cannot
be denied:

> You have turned my mourning into dancing;
>> you have taken off my sackcloth
>> and clothed me with joy . . . (Ps. 30:11)

The prophet Isaiah, at the beginning and at the end, lines out *the drama of
loss and the possibility of restoration.*

> At the beginning, loss:

>> *Instead* of perfume there will be a stench;
>>> and *instead* of a sash, a rope;
>> and *instead* of well-set hair, baldness;
>>> and *instead* of a rich robe, a binding of sackcloth;
>>> *instead* of beauty, shame. (Isa. 3:24)

> At the end, hope:

>> . . . to give them a garland *instead* of ashes,
>>> the oil of gladness *instead* of mourning,
>>>> the mantle of praise *instead* of a faint spirit. (Isa. 61:3)

The second set of "insteads" is as crucial to prophetic preaching as is the first
set. By the time the abandonment is acknowledged and the silence is broken,
we are at the front edge of new historical possibility.

CHAPTER 5

The Burst of Newness amid Waiting

IT TURNS OUT that the prophets were right about loss. The destruction of Jerusalem and the deportation that followed made clear, according to the tradition, that a people out of sync with God's purposes in policy and in practice comes under judgment. The symmetry of "being out of sync" applies, eventually, even to God's special, privileged, chosen people (see Amos 3:2). The status of "chosen" provides no "pass" on that symmetrical uncompromising covenantal arrangement. The loss was visible in the body politic and in the theological symbolism of Israel and its special city.

And the loss had to be grieved. It was, as I have suggested, grieved,

—by Israel,
—in anticipation by the prophets, and
—by YHWH in the utterance of the prophets.

I

The loss was, so the prophets declared, inevitable in the purview of the covenantal theology of Sinai and Deuteronomy. Through the imaginative interpretation of Sinai in the tradition of Deuteronomy, the covenant came to be a tight, symmetrical system of quid pro quo. In the formulation of Deuteronomy, if the *quo* was obedience, the *quid* was covenant blessing; conversely, when the *quo* was disobedience, the *quid* was covenant curse. According to the prophetic tradition, the *quo* was in fact disobedience, whether a violation of holiness or an affront of injustice. Either way, it was a failure in listening and obeying:

> Yet the LORD warned Israel and Judah by every prophet and every
> seer, saying, "Turn from your evil ways and keep my commandments
> and my statutes, in accordance with all the law that I commanded
> your ancestors and that I sent to you by my servants the prophets."
> They would not listen but were stubborn, as their ancestors had
> been, who did not believe in the LORD their God. They despised his
> statutes, and his covenant that he made with their ancestors, and the
> warnings that he gave them. They went after false idols and became
> false; they followed the nations that were around them, concern-
> ing whom the LORD had commanded them that they should not
> do as they did. They rejected all the commandments of the LORD
> their God . . . Therefore the LORD was very angry with Israel and
> removed them out of his sight; none was left but the tribe of Judah
> alone. Judah also did not keep the commandments of the LORD
> their God but walked in the customs that Israel had introduced. The
> LORD rejected all the descendants of Israel; he punished them and
> gave them into the hand of plunderers, until he had banished them
> from his presence. (2 Kgs. 17:13-20)

The history of Israel and Judah is summarized as being unbearably out of sync. All of that, according to Sinai.

II

When Israel grieved its loss, however, there was no more mileage in Sinai. It would do no good, substantively or emotionally, to hammer any longer at the symmetry of quid pro quo. In the post-587 season of grief, the prophets continued to appeal to old tradition. But most remarkably, they now were pressed by circumstance and by their acute pastoral sensibility to go behind the Sinai tradition to the prior (I do not say "earlier") traditions of Genesis.[1] It would serve no purpose any longer to accent the conditionality of covenant when Israel had blatantly refused those conditions. And if that were all that was available, there would be nothing further to say.

But the prophets are endlessly resourceful in their poetic imagination and in their appropriation of the tradition. They found, in the traditions of Gen-esis, ample funding for something new to say to Israel in its loss and in its grief. The Genesis traditions, of course, provide two rich themes for fresh utterance. First, the theme of creation attests that YHWH has the capacity to form new worlds out of the chaos at hand. There was no need to speak of *creatio ex nihilo* because the prophets could readily find a contemporary chaos (*tohu webohu*) in the exile that surely was an immediate instance of acute chaos (Jer. 4:22-26). Most explicitly, Isaiah brings the interpretive theme of chaos to the crisis of exile:

> For thus says the LORD,
>   who created the heavens
>   (he is God!).
> who formed the earth and made it
>   (he established it;
> he did not create it a chaos,
>   he formed it to be inhabited!):
> I am the LORD, and there is no other.
> I did not speak in secret,
>   in a land of darkness;
> I did not say to the offspring of Jacob,
>   "Seek me in chaos."
> I the LORD speak the truth,
>   I declare what is right. (Isa. 45:18-19)

This accent is reinforced in Isaiah by appeal to the flood tradition, where the exile is likened to the flood, and the end of the flood with the divine verdict of, "Never again," is a reassurance to the exiles:

> This is like the days of Noah to me:
>   Just as I swore that the waters of Noah
>   would *never again* go over the earth,
> so I have sworn that I will not be angry with you
>   and will not rebuke you. (Isa. 54:9; see Gen. 9:15)

The creator's capacity to work a newness, unencumbered by conditionality and unassisted by any other power, becomes a joyous assertion that YHWH will work a newness right in the midst of Israel's most dire circumstance of grief. That newness is articulated in many images; the important point, however, is that it is freely and singularly enacted by YHWH without respect to the "qualification" of Israel or the assistance of other gods. (On the later, see Isaiah 41:26-29).

Second, the creation theme is matched in the book of Genesis by the divine promise to the ancestors, a tradition that is commonly taken as an unconditional intention from God without resort to any prior "obedience" on the part of Abraham and his family.[2] The theme of divine promise saturates the ancestral narratives of Genesis 12–50, a promise that variously concerns name, progeny, land, and blessing to the nations (see Genesis 12:1-3; 18:18; 22:18; 26:4; 28:13-15). Abraham and his family are offered irrefutable evidence that YHWH, by decree, can enact a *novum* in world history. And from that memory the prophets dare to assert that in the failure of the exile, YHWH will enact a *novum* before the very eyes of Israel. That *novum* will defy the host empire and bring YHWH's people to joy and well-being in their homeland.

The specific enactment of a *novum* without antecedent is the gift of an heir to the ancestral mother who is barren and completely without prospect of a child. In each subsequent generation of the ancestors, the divine promise is always again in jeopardy without an heir:

> Now Sarai was *barren*; she had no child. (Gen. 11:30)

> Isaac prayed to the LORD for his wife, because she was *barren* . . .
>   (Gen. 25:21)

> When the LORD saw that Leah was unloved, he opened her womb;
>   but Rachel was *barren*. (Gen. 29:31)

(And of course the motif "barren mother" is continued with reference to mother Hannah (1 Sam. 1:2, 10-11) and mother Elizabeth (Luke 1:7). Each birth that extends the divine promise to the next generation is given at the last moment by the inexplicable power and fidelity of YHWH. The theme of barrenness to birth is explicitly utilized by Isaiah in a declaration of new possibility for the displaced community:

> Sing, O barren one who did not bear;
>   burst into song and shout,
>   you who have not been in labor!
> For the children of the desolate women will be more
>   than the children of her that is married, says the LORD.
> Enlarge the site of your tent,
>   and let the curtains of your habitations be stretched out;
> do not hold back; lengthen your cords

and strengthen your stakes.
For you will spread out to the right and to the left,
    and your descendents will possess the nations
    and will settle the desolate towns. (Isa. 54:1-3)

The barren one, mother Sarah, now becomes barren, hopeless Israel. This barren one will surpass the Babylonian empire ("She that is married") in blessing and fruitfulness from YHWH. The ancestral traditions of "barrenness to birth" permit the prophets to declare new possibility for Israel in its grief and despair.

Most specifically, the birth announcement to Abraham and Sarah in Genesis 18:1-16a may be taken as the pivot point of new possibility in the narrative. Claus Westermann judges that this was an antecedent family saga, but it is the narrative that exhibits the family saga as a vehicle for divine promise:

> Here—and only here—does the circle of the promise narrative
> coincide completely with the circle of the family narrative. Here,
> therefore, we have the crucial starting point for the transformation
> of the cycle of family sagas into a saga cycle defined by the promise
> to Abraham. . . . This narrative describes an archetypal experience
> of distress and its alleviation through God's miraculous interven-
> tion. It remains totally within the realm of the family, be it noted,
> however, that this is here the realm of crucial events. It has the same
> significance that deliverance from pursuit through God's miraculous
> intervention had for the nomadic group. Because of this significance
> it was recounted and handed down. Here we find the reality and tra-
> dition of deliverance, liberation, and redemption in the full theologi-
> cal sense of the word.[3]

In this narrative, the "strangers" arrive who turn out to be a representatives of YHWH. They come to Abraham and Sarah, who are "old, advanced in age; it had ceased to be with Sarah after the manner of women" (v. 11). In the midst of the bewildered, embarrassed resistance of Sarah, the Lord said, "Why did Sarah laugh, and say, 'Shall I indeed bear a child, now that I am old?' Is anything too wonderful for the LORD? At the set time I will return to you in due season, and Sarah shall have a son." (vv. 13-14). The pivot of the narrative is in the word "too wonderful" that can also be rendered "too difficult" or "impossible." The question posed by the visitor is whether YHWH, in making the promise, can go beyond perceived possibility to do what is commonly judged to be impossible. The question hangs over the narratives of Genesis. In each generation, it is "not possible" for a barren mother in Israel to have a son as an heir who will keep the divine promise to Israel alive. And in each generation, the "impossible" happens. The barren mother has a son and the promise persists!

The question always haunts Israel. That same question haunts Israel in exile: Can YHWH create, yet again, a new history for Israel, after the old history has come to a dismal end? Here we are at the deepest theological question of biblical faith—is the God of faith contained within and informed by what the world knows to be possible? Or is it within the capacity of God to create a newness that defies the categories of the "possible" that are commonly and reasonably accepted in the world?

Karl Barth, in the second volume of his great *Church Dogmatics*, faces the issue of what is "real" and what is "possible." It is ordinary, according to any common rationality, to begin with what is *possible*; and then to judge what is *real* on the basis of the *possible*. Thus if it is not "possible," it cannot be "real." Barth's great epistemological nerve is to invert the process. He insists that "the real" comes first in the mystery of God. Then he asks the question: (1) How far God in His revelation is free for us, that is, free to reveal himself to us, free to be our God without at the same time ceasing to be God the Lord; and (2) how far God in His revelation is also free in us, that is, free to deal with us as His own, who belong to Him.[4] And answers:

> This second question at once includes and answers the other ques-
> tion; how far in God's revelation we become free for Him, so that
> He can be manifest to us. The question about the freedom of God
> for man and in man is the one which points most comprehensively
> and decisively to the two answers we have to take up here. God is
> not prevented either by His own deity or by our humanity and sin-
> fulness from being our God and having intercourse with us as with
> His own. On the contrary, He is free for us and in us.[5]

And this leads to Barth's verdict on which his entire testimony rests:

> It concerns the possibility of revelation: How is the encounter of His
> revelation with man possible in the freedom of God? This second
> question, too, has it propriety and its necessity. It is the question of
> interpretation, the question of exegesis, which must certainly follow
> the question of fact, the question of the text. But it can only follow
> it. It must not claim to precede it.[6]

Barth's insistence that the issue of "possibility" must not claim to precede the question of "reality" is crucial. And because God is free, much is possible with God that would not otherwise be possible.

It is useful to recognize, in our own context, that when faith is contained within modern rationality, there is a rejection of the God who can "do the impossible." The present casting of that rejection concerns "an interventionist God" who violates our notion of the possible. But, says Barth, that is exactly the wrong starting place. Israel never makes such a generic argument. Rather it focuses upon narrative specificity to name the moment of newness and surprise that violates the "possible." The issue is, of course, acute amid our modernity. We should not think, however, that it was so very different in the ancient world, for they also were practitioners of common sense observation and learned what was possible in their world. And surely in the displacement of the exile they judged what was possible, and they judged with shrewd political sense that it was not possible to overthrow or escape the Babylonian empire. There were, they concluded, some things that were "too hard" for YHWH.

The question left by the narrative of Genesis 18 lingers over the Bible. It is a question about the freedom of God that we seek to ponder without any recourse to crude supernaturalism. The temptation to such crude supernaturalism, however, is matched by a temptation to reduce God to an echo and reflection of common sense rationality that does away with the issue of God's freedom.[7]

Thus the question of the "impossible" runs directly into the New Testament:

- In the annunciation narrative with which Luke begins his Gospel account, Gabriel concludes his birth announcement with in this way:

    For nothing will be *impossible* with God. (Luke 1:37)

There can be no doubt that Luke intentionally echoes the Genesis narrative. The son given to Mary is "impossible" and will continue the promise of God.

- In the narrative of the "rich, young ruler," Jesus exclaims that the rescue of a rich person is exceedingly difficult. In response to the bewildered question of verse 26, Jesus responds:

    What is *impossible* for mortals is *possible* for God.
    (Luke 18:27)

The declaration breaks God out of the humanly possible for the sake of a God-given new possibility.

- In Luke 22:42, on the Mount of Olive, Jesus prays:

> Father, if you are willing, remove this cup from me; yet, not my
> will but yours be done. (Luke 22:42)

But in the parallel in Mark 14:35, our term is utilized to yield the petition of
Jesus:

> . . . he threw himself on the ground and prayed that, if it were
> *possible*, the hour might pass from him. He said, "Abba, Father,
> for you all things are *possible*; remove this cup from me; yet, not
> what I want, but what you want." (Mark 14:35-36)

Again, the narrative pushes "the possible" for God. In this case, apparently, the removal of "the hour" is not a possibility for God. Or in the Lucan
account, God is not "willing."

It is clear in all these texts that the old question from Genesis 18:13 lingers.
In each new articulation, Israel must ask again in wonderment if God, in
God's freedom, can push beyond ordinary "possibility" to the "impossible."
The Genesis wonder of the birth of an heir to Sarah and Abraham is reiterated
in the recital of Hebrews 11 where it is asserted: "By faith he received power
of procreation, even though he was too old—and Sarah herself was barren—
because he considered him faithful who had promised. Therefore from one
person, and this one as good as dead, descendants were born, as many as the
stars of the heavens and as the innumerable grains of sand by the seashore"
(Heb. 11:11-12). Here the term "possible" is not used, but the point is the
same. The tradition of faith continues to be dazzled by specific memories, in
narrative form, of instances in which the "impossibility of God" has overrid-
den the "possibility" of human wisdom. Israel clings to those memories that
exhibit God's faithful power beyond our expectation or explanation.

III

The doxological tradition of Israel that issues in praise and thanks offers an
inventory of "miracles," that is, of narrative memories of the exhibits of God's
power for the impossible. Here I cite three representative recitals, in variant
forms, of that rich tradition of doxology:

1. Psalm 145 is a doxology that situates the sweep of all creation under
the governing fidelity of YHWH. Verses 14-20 summarize YHWH's

characteristic actions of sustenance and care. But before that, the introduction of verses 4-7 offers a rich vocabulary of "miracle" that celebrates the stream of impossibilities enacted by YHWH:

> One generation shall laud your works to another,
>   and shall declare your mighty acts.
> On the glorious splendor of your majesty,
>   and on your wondrous works, I will meditate.
> The might of your awesome deeds shall be proclaimed,
>   and I will declare your greatness.
> They shall celebrate the fame of your abundant goodness,
>   and shall sing aloud of your righteousness. (Ps. 145:4-7)

This praise of Israel includes reference to "your works," "your mighty acts," "your wondrous works," "your awesome deeds," "your abundant good-ness," and "your righteousness." Each of these terms merits close attention and carries its own nuance. As the terms cluster together, however, they have a common force. Each of them and all of them together provide the substance of faith which Israel sings back to YHWH. When the psalm begins its more detailed enumeration, all the acts constitute YHWH's inexplicable way in the world that is marked by reliability and generosity that is without parallel (vv. 14-20). Thus the way of YHWH in the world is seen in its "glorious splen-dor (vv. 5, 12), "greatness" (v. 6), "faithfulness" (v. 14), and "graciousness" (v. 14), plus the stylized formulation of verses 8-9 that is rooted in the old formula of Exodus 34:6-7. YHWH's transformative manifestations defy all explanation and evoke praise that is exuberant and boundless.

2. Psalm 107 is cast in the very different style of thanksgiving.[8] In its thanks, Israel may become quite specific. In this rendition, we are offered four characteristic cases of YHWH's transformative capacity:

- Rescue from desert wandering (vv. 4-9);
- Emancipation from prison (vv. 10-16);
- Deliverance from sickness (vv. 17-22);
- Rescue from a dangerous storm (vv. 23-32).

In each highly stylized case, there is (a) a statement of the crisis, (b) a cry to YHWH, and (c) an immediate response of rescue by YHWH. What interests us, however, is the conclusion in each case wherein the rescued are enjoined: "Let them thank the LORD for his steadfast love, for his *wonderful works* to humankind (v. 8; see vv. 15, 21, 31-32)." Each such act is identified as an exhibit of divine fidelity (*ḥesed*) and as one of YHWH's "wondrous deeds." The term for this is *niphle'oth*, from the same root as the term in Genesis 18:14). Thus praise and thanks are due to YHWH for the "impossibilities" that YHWH has performed that have given Israel new life amid its deep distress. Such divine performance can only evoke praise and thanks. The speaker of the psalm never doubts that YHWH can do such acts, for Israel has experienced such wonders in its own life.

3. Psalm 136 is a summary doxology that narrates the entire historical memory of Israel from creation (vv. 4-9) to the arrival in the land of promise (vv. 21-23). The distinguishing mark of this recital, however, is the recurring reiteration of the term "steadfast love" and the crediting of each historical memory to the faithful action of YHWH. These several remembered events are not just historical happenings. They are articulations and enactments of YHWH's covenantal fidelity. The term "impossible" ("wondrous") is not used here, but it is surely implied. The history of Israel is a history of miracles in which YHWH's faithful power cracks open all the categories of human history for the sake of Israel's well-being and for the shalom of the world. In sum, the psalm is one more answer to the haunting question of Genesis 18: "Yes, YHWH can do the impossible" YHWH can do what is too wonderful! YHWH can do what is too difficult!

IV

I have taken this long to exposit the question of Genesis 18 because it is the question that surfaces each time Israel ponders its future in the midst of its loss, grief, and dismay. Each time it does such pondering, it wonders and waits again, trusting but not knowing if this is a time for yet another divine "impossibility."[9] So it is that in the nadir of its displacement after the destruction of Jerusalem, the question surfaced yet again. It was a question sometimes answered by Israel in resignation, as in Isaiah 40:27, 49:14, and Jeremiah 8:20. But it was also a lingering question that remained open and unanswered. It was the task and the opportunity of the prophets, the ones with poetic imagination in ancient Israel, to give a forceful "yes" to Israel in its displacement: Yes, YHWH can and will work an impossibility on behalf of the future well-being of Israel. I accent the point because very much of our "prophetic preaching" is defined by and limited to urgent social action pleading. It cannot be emphasized too strongly, in my judgment, that prophetic preaching is the enactment of hope in contexts of loss and grief. It is the declaration that God can enact a *novum* in our very midst, even when we judge that to be impossible.

I suggest that such a performance of prophetic preaching may be particularly appropriate in the circumstance of our society. I say that only after having said all of the foregoing about judgment being out of sync, and about loss and grief. When the denial of guilt and grief and loss has been penetrated, prophetic preaching has a new task. In the prophetic books themselves, the literature moves, every time, through judgment and grief to hope-filled possibility. The book of Ezekiel is symmetrically arranged so that chapters 32–48, the latter half of the book, concerns divine possibility. In the book of Isaiah, the matter is formulated according to the familiar hypothesis of "Second Isaiah" (40–55) and less directly in "Third Isaiah" (56–66). In the book of Jeremiah, the matter is more complex. But after the letter to the exiles in Jeremiah 29:1-7, and certainly after the oracle to Baruch in 45:1-5, the literature moves to hope.

Recent canonical study, most notably in the work of Ronald Clements, is clear that the move toward hope in prophetic literature is not an add-on or a belated after-thought.[10] It is, rather, characteristically intrinsic to the prophetic message. It is clear in the prophetic books that the work is not completed until the depth of judgment, loss, and grief is turned to new possibility. *Mutatis mutandis*, it is clear that prophetic preaching, even in our own time, is not completed until the depth of judgment, loss, and grief is turned toward new possibility. Such a turn, however, is not automatic. Nor does it mean, I believe, that we must end in hope in every utterance, as the ancient poets did not. Hope can, of course, be spoken too soon. And when spoken too soon, it may too soon overcome the loss and short-circuit the indispensible embrace of guilt and loss. The new possibility is always on the horizon for prophetic preachers. But good sense and theological courage are required to know when to say what. No doubt among us there is a common temptation to rush to the good news. The poet unmistakably arrived there. But there is ample reason to recognize that they did not rush to the point.

The pivot point of my exposition will be the extended material of Jeremiah 32.[11] This extended passage begins with the familiar narrative concerning Jeremiah's purchase of the family property. The final verse of that narrative turns the specific real-estate transaction into a sweeping covenantal promise: "For thus says the LORD of hosts, the God of Israel; Houses and fields and vineyards shall again be bought in this land" (v. 15) (see Mark 10). That promise, moreover, becomes the launching pad for the remainder of the chapter that consists in Jeremiah's prayer (vv. 16-25) and YHWH's responsive oracle (vv. 26-44). I begin with this passage because of the remarkable fact that both the prayer and the oracle open with the use of our term from Genesis 18, "too wonderful": "Ah LORD God! It is you who made the heavens and the earth by your great power and by your outstretched arm! Nothing is *too hard* for you" (v. 17).

"See, I am the LORD, the God of all flesh; is anything *too hard* for me?" (v. 27). The double use of the term places this latter text in the orbit of the narrative of Genesis 18 and indicates that the question of Genesis 18 continues to preoccupy Israel in its exile.

The long prayer of Jeremiah thus begins with a doxology to the creator, plus the verdict of the same verse (v. 17). Here the question of "too wonderful" has become a settled claim and conviction. It is as though Jeremiah, in his prayer, must give a reminder or an assurance to YHWH that YHWH is indeed free and is not confined by the conventional limits of the facts on the ground.

In tracing the impossibilities of YHWH, the prayer moves through three themes that reflect Israel's lived experience. First, Jeremiah offers a long doxology that celebrates YHWH's faithful, gracious power (vv. 18-19), tracing the history of Israel from the Exodus to the promised land (vv. 20-23a). The entire history of Israel is presented as an "impossibility" that YHWH has wrought. And indeed, it was impossible for the slaves to depart from Egypt and impossible that this emergent community could occupy the new land. That memory cannot be taken for granted but must evoke awe and gratitude. Second, Jeremiah's prayer reflects the prophetic conviction that Israel has been out of sync with YHWH and has received the inescapable pay-back (vv. 23b-24). These verses, governed by three rhetorical markers, offer a standard prophetic speech of judgment:

> But . . . they did not listen;
> They did nothing.
> Therefore . . . disaster
> Behold . . . famine, pestilence, war.

These verses are also governed by the initial "too wonderful" in verse 17. It would be "too hard" for YHWH to act against YHWH's own chosen people and chosen city. By any standard, that could not be done. Except that YHWH is not tame in such a way.

Third, the prayer culminates in verse 25 with an adversative "yet" (*waw* consecutive): "Yet you . . ." Beyond the initial memory of rescue and beyond the present alienation ending in destruction, there is one more "impossibility." The prophet, in his prayer, quotes YHWH from verse 15 back to YHWH: "Yet you, O LORD God, have said to me, 'Buy the field for money and get witnesses'—though the city has been given into the hands of the Chaldeans" (v. 25). The quote derives from the modest imperative of v. 9, "Buy my field," together with the divine promise of verse 15. Taken together, the two statements of verses 9 and 15 now issue into a huge imperative that contains a promise. The imperative/promise contrasts the fact on the ground of the Chaldeans. It would be "impossible" for an Israelite to value land held by the Babylonians. But the impossibility of YHWH violates that Babylonian "fact" and so creates a new future.

The three "scenes" in the prayer correspond to the three seasons of Israel's life: *initial success*, *disastrous judgment*, and now, *possibility beyond the Chaldeans*. Each step of the way is an impossibility, impossible to go from Egypt to the land, impossible to have chosenness violated, and now impossible to recover. It is the impossible recovery that occupies the present prophetic proclamation.

The oracle of YHWH (vv. 26-44) corresponds to the prophetic prayer of verses 16-25. The initial claim of YHWH, like the initial address of the prophet (v. 27 as v. 17) begins with an appeal to the power of the creator and then asks the question about "too difficult." Here it is a question, but it is a rhetorical question that the following verses answer. Clearly nothing is too difficult for the creator God. The text is a rumination on two impossibilities. First, verses 28-35, introduced by "therefore," traverse the prophetic themes of Israel's covenantal failure and YHWH's judgment. It is that uncontested reality that brings us to the pivot point of verse 26. "Now therefore" at the beginning sets a clear division between that failed past and present-future prospects. Verse 36 yet again fully acknowledges the failed state of Jerusalem. The "behold" of verse 37, echoing and contrasting with the same term in verse 24, opens future prospects with a series of first person divine resolves:

> I am going to gather,
> I will bring them,
> I will give them one heart,
> I will make an everlasting covenant,
> I will put my fear in them,
> I will rejoice in doing good,
> I will plant them.

This is not too hard for YHWH! YHWH will enact the newness against all circumstance. The recital of divine resolves includes within it the promise of an "everlasting covenant" with its guaranteed "never" (v. 40) and the covenant formula (v. 39) that emerges in Israel precisely in its displacement. It is in exile that the covenant formula repeatedly occurs.[12] It is in the nadir of failure that YHWH makes new promises.

The core promises in verses 37-44 are supplemented by more guarantees in verses 42-44. The formulation of "just as . . . so" in verse 42 holds together the action of divine judgment now resolved and the action of coming "good fortune" now promised. It is the same God who brought disaster who now brings good. Or in the governing formula of Jeremiah, it is the same Lord of the covenant who has "plucked up and torn down" who will now "plant and build" (Jer. 1:10; 31:27-28). The supplement includes the verdict echoing verses 15 and 25:

> Fields shall be bought in this land of which you are saying, It is a desolation, without human beings or animals . . . Fields shall be bought for money, and deeds shall be signed and sealed and witnessed, in the land of Benjamin, in the places around Jerusalem, and in the cities of Judah, of the hill country, of the Shephelah, and of the Negeb; for I will restore their fortunes, says the LORD. (vv. 43-44)

The resolve of YHWH contradicts circumstance and works a newness that is inexplicable, except for the deep fidelity of YHWH that moves beyond alienation and disaster.

V

In what follows, I propose that the question of Genesis 18 and the certitude of Jeremiah 32:17 (informed by the witness of verses 27ff.) is the prism of the prophetic preaching of hope. Such voicing of hope is done in poetic idiom because the prophet must say what goes beyond all the evidence. Thus the prophet does not offer plans and blueprints of specificity. Rather the hope that is voiced is lyrical and open, but with enough concreteness that it gives ground for the future. In what follows, I will consider in turn each of the three "great prophets" who give voice to hope with confidence in the God who is not hemmed in by circumstance.

A. *Ezekiel* is a prophet who likely belonged to the influential priesthood of the Jerusalem temple. Consequently, he viewed the life of his people through the prism of the temple and the requirement of holiness. The loss he grieves includes the pollution of the temple that caused the departure of YHWH from the temple (8-10). It is not a surprise, then, that as Ezekiel conjured the future of Israel amid exile, he imagined and anticipated a full restoration of the Jerusalem temple that is to be symmetrical and rightly decorated as a suitable place for the return of YHWH's presence (45). The characterization of an adequate temple amid a properly ordered promised land caused the book of Ezekiel to end with the affirmation that the restored city is now named "The LORD is There" (48:35). In the midst of that acute absence of YHWH,

Ezekiel can offer hope for the restored presence of YHWH, and therefore the reconstitution of a viable life in the city and in the land. We learn from Ezekiel, as we may learn with each prophet, that the particular shape of hope is to some great extent dictated by the prism of particular experience, theological commitment, and social interest. Temple presence is the defining hope for Ezekiel the prophet.

But along the way to "temple hope," Ezekiel lingers over other images and other possibilities for Jerusalem's future. I will mention three of these.

1. In Ezekiel 34, the prophetic judgment is that Israel is "scattered" (sent into exile) because of bad "shepherds" (kings). That is, kings in Jerusalem did not practice covenantal obedience and so produced displacement. Verses 3-4 detail the failure of greedy royal power. The text turns abruptly in verse 11, as though YHWH has made a new resolve. The turn from verses 2-10 to the promise in verses 11ff. is characteristic of the rhetoric of disruption in the prophets, a rhetorical disruption that corresponds to the lived disjunction of the displaced Israelites. Now, in verse 11, YHWH declares that YHWH's own self will be king (shepherd) in Israel, and will do the covenantal work that the Davidic kings had refused to do. Verses 11-16 are dominated by first-person verbs of YHWH that contrast with the repeated, "you, you, you" of verses 3-4. YHWH will do restorative work:

> I will seek you;
> I will rescue;
> I will bring them out;
> I will gather;
> I will bring them into their own land;
> I will feed them;
> I will feed them with good pasture;
> I will make them lie down;
> I will seek the lost;
> I will bring back the strayed;
> I will bind up the injured;
> I will strengthen the weak;
> I will feed them with justice.

In time to come, YHWH will do what kings are supposed to do; YHWH will utilize power for the enhancement of the community.

That recital of first-person resolve receives a reprise in verses 25-29 wherein the scope of restoration is moved even beyond the people to the well-being of all creation:

> I will make a covenant of shalom;
> I will banish wild animals;
> I will make them and their region . . . a blessing;
> I will send down showers;
> I will break the bars of their yoke;
> I will save them;
> I will provide them a splendid vegetation.

The outcome will be a restored covenant that yields security and prosperity. The text concludes with two synonymous variations on the covenant formula:

> They shall know that I, the LORD their God, am with them, and that they, the house of Israel, are my people, says the Lord GOD. (v. 30)

> You are my sheep, the sheep of my pasture and I am your God, says the LORD God. (v. 31)

Two matters may be observed in this remarkable resolve. First, it is anticipated that this restoration will be the direct work of YHWH without human agency. The text does not speculate on the means for such restoration. Except that in verses 23-24 the assumption of direct divine agency is modified by reference to "my servant David." It is to be noted, however, that the anticipated David will be a "prince" and not a king. The role of king is retained for YHWH's own self. These two verses, in any case, move in the direction of political realism about human agency.

Second, while the statement is not lined out in poetic meter, we may notice that the words of the prophet do not describe procedure or blueprint, but remain at an elusive level of possibility. Such a mode of discourse is, of course, congruent with the earlier prophetic utterances we have considered. This promise is indeed an act of imagination wherein the prophet (and YHWH) imagined and anticipated a world out beyond present reality. Indeed, prophetic possibility refuses to be contained in present possibility. It does not pause to ask if the anticipated scenario is "too hard" for YHWH, for with YHWH, "Nothing is too hard" (Jer. 32:17), not even a restoration of people, city, and creation. The coming world of YHWH on earth is a gift of *shalom* that will take realistic political shape.

2. Ezekiel 36:22-32 offers a second utterance of YHWH concerning the coming restoration of the house of Israel. Again the promise is dominated by divine resolve: "I will sanctify my great name, which has been profaned among

the nations, and which you have profaned among them; and the nations shall know that I am the LORD, says the LORD God, when through you I display my holiness before their eyes" (v. 23). The promise is not first of all about the future of Israel; it is about the future of YHWH. YHWH's name (reputation) has been "profaned" by the gross actions of Israel; YHWH must undertake restorative action for YHWH's own self. The odd and defining reality of the covenant, however, is that YHWH's self-restoration can only be accomplished or exhibited through Israel's restoration. Thus it is "through you." For that reason, what follows after verse 23 is a divine resolve to restore Israel:

> I will take you;
> I will gather you;
> I will bring you;
> I will sprinkle;
> I will cleanse you;
> I will give you a new heart;
> I will put a new spirit in you;
> I will remove;
> I will put my spirit;
> I will make you follow;
> I will save you;
> I will summon the grain;
> I will make it abundant;
> I will make the fruit of the tree . . .

Again, restoration of Israel, perforce, includes restoration of creation to its full fruitful function; again, the rhetoric is imaginative and without explanation; again, YHWH is the direct actor without any human agent. It is YHWH's resolve, declared in the abyss of displacement, in order to generate for Israel a new world.

The remarkable feature of this promise is that it is framed by verses 22 and 33 with the declaration that "It is not for your sake." The Ezekiel tradition is so fixed upon YHWH's awesome holiness that it contains nothing of pathos or emotive inclination toward Israel. Israel's future well-being is a by-product of YHWH's self-regard. The well-being of Israel is the only way YHWH has to exhibit the full, splendid sovereignty of YHWH to the nations. But it is an inescapable by-product that is very certain, because the God of Ezekiel will finally not be mocked or diminished, or trivialized, even by Israel's self-destructive conduct. The ground for future possibility in Israel is YHWH's self-regard that has been unbearably cheapened by Israel.

3. The vision of 37:1-4 is familiar to us. Ezekiel is led by YHWH to ponder over the lifeless "dry bones" of Israel in exile. The circumstance of exilic despair is voiced in verse 11: "Our bones are dried up, and our hope is lost; we are cut off completely" (v. 11). That voiced despair, however, is contradicted and overcome by divine resolve. The status of "dried up" and "cut off" is countered in the text by the repeated use of the term *ruah* (breath, wind, spirit). The repeated use of the term reflects the notion that the body of any creature, including human creatures and including Israel, completely depends upon YHWH's breath to animate and bring to life:

> When you hide your face, they are dismayed;
> when you take away their *breath*, they die and return to their dust.
> When you send forth your *spirit*, they are created;
> and you renew the face of the ground. (Ps. 104:29-30)

Thus the promise of YHWH in Ezekiel 37:5, "I will cause breath to enter you, and you shall live" (v. 5), is reminiscent of Genesis 2:7 and the initial human creation. This text utilizes the language of creation in order to reflect upon the recreation of Israel in displacement after it has been "dried up, and . . . cut off." Israel itself had "no breath" (v. 8), but breath is given, breath that Israel cannot possess or generate for itself because can only receive as YHWH's singular gift. The vision of Ezekiel is of a newly breathed-on Israel that now has life again, that is beyond the deathliness of displacement. That breath, of course, cannot be coerced from YHWH; it can only be given. And now, says Ezekiel, YHWH is ready and eager to give breath in order that Israel may live again.

The commentary on the vision in verses 12-14 continues with the imagery of restoration from the dead with reference to "opening your graves." Verse 13, however, brings the imagery to the historical reality of Israel, namely, return to the land from which they had been deported. The final verse draws the metaphorical and historical terms together: "'I will put my spirit within you, and you shall live, and I will place you on your own soil; then you shall know that I, the LORD, have spoken and will act,' says the LORD." Using the imagery of recreation and resurrection retains for YHWH alone the initiative for Israel's future. It also makes clear that Israel's future is an "impossibility" that YHWH can perform. Jon Levenson has helpfully traced the way in which "resurrection" is "restoration" as "the ultimate victory of the God of life." Congruent with Ezekiel's vision of the temple, Levenson sees the temple as "the antipode of Sheol":[13]

> In the Temple, instead of want, they found surfeit; instead of abandonment, care; instead of pollution, purity; instead of victimization,

justice; instead of threat, security; instead of vulnerability, inviolability; instead of change, fixity; and instead of temporality, eternity. If this sounds like the World-to-Come or the Garden of Eden of rabbinic tradition, or the heaven of Christianity, that is surely no coincidence, for the Temple is the source of much of the imagery out of which much of those ideas grew.[14]

It is clear that Ezekiel's vision is no commonplace of historical possibility. It is precisely an "impossibility" wrought only by YHWH that emerged in the midst of the exilic abyss. YHWH has the capacity to enact a *novum* that is commensurate with the *novum* of creation. This is indeed the God of life who acts for this people that had forfeited its chance for life. It is no wonder that in Ezekiel 36 the prophet avers that such an act of restoration for Israel redounds to the honor of YHWH.

The concluding verses of chapter 37 reiterate the promises of the foregoing but with significantly different nuance (vv. 24-27):

- The future will be a David-governed future, accenting the emerging "messianism" of the exilic period. In verse 25, the future David is called a "prince," as in 34:24, but in verse 24 is termed a "king." The double usage indicates some ambiguity about the role of a future David in the rule of YHWH.
- The renewed covenant is "an everlasting covenant" (v. 26; see 16:60). The promised covenant contrasts with the prior covenant that manifestly had been broken via the exile.
- The passage reiterates the "covenant formula" that recurs in the exile: "My dwelling place shall be with them; and I will be their God, and they shall be my people" (v. 27).
- The final assurance is holiness for Israel that is commensurate with YHWH's "holy sanctuary" now reestablished in Jerusalem. The final modifier, "forevermore" reiterates the term from verse 26. Holiness is restored to the people and the city that had been polluted, making possible the reentry of YHWH into the city and YHWH's continuing residence there. All of these phrases, cumulatively, offer Israel a remarkable basis for the future that s not derived from any present facts on the ground, but only from the promissory fidelity of YHWH that wells up, via the prophet, at the nadir of displacement.

B. We have seen in *Jeremiah* (30:12-17 and 30:20) that the poet traces the anguish YHWH has over Israel that will lead to new interventions of YHWH toward Israel in exile. It is common to recognize that in the book of Jeremiah the proclamation of new possibility for Israel from YHWH is clustered especially in chapters 30-31, commonly called "The Book of Comfort" (see 30:2), perhaps originally an independent scroll. In these chapters (and the addendum of 32-33), the recurring promise of YHWH is that YHWH will "restore the fortunes" of Israel, that is, reverse the circumstance of death and displacement (30:3, 18; 32:44; 33:11, 26).

Jeremiah was from the village priesthood of Anathoth (1:1). Unlike Ezekiel who was of the urban, pedigreed priesthood, Jeremiah no doubt reflects a very different kind of priesthood that was devoted not to the temple but to Torah teaching. It is for that reason that the book of Jeremiah has significant connections to the tradition of Deuteronomy, the great scroll of covenant fidelity. Whereas in Ezekiel the ground for YHWH's restoration of Israel is the recovery of *YHWH's holiness*, in the Jeremiah tradition, the ground for such action is *YHWH's pathos*. YHWH is deeply moved toward Israel and acts accordingly. In Jeremiah, there is little reference to the temple, but there is no doubt that the city of Jerusalem, in this offer of hope, will be restored and rebuilt. The three-fold "again" of 31:4-5 anticipates recovery:

> Again I will build you, and you shall be built,
> > O virgin Israel!
> Again you shall take your tambourines,
> > and go forth in the dance of the merrymakers.
> Again you shall plant vineyards
> > on the mountains of Samaria;
> the planters shall plant,
> > and shall enjoy the fruit.
> For there shall be a day when the sentinels will call
> > in the hill country of Ephraim:
> "Come, let us go up to Zion,
> > to the LORD our God." (31:4-6)

The "scattered" (exiles) will be "gathered" into a recovered community of profound joy:

> "He who scattered Israel will gather him,
> > and will keep him as a shepherd a flock."
> . . . .
> They shall come and sing aloud on the height of Zion,
> > and they shall be radiant over the goodness of the LORD,
> over the grain, the wine, and the oil,

and over the young of the flock and the herd;
their life shall become like a watered garden,
    and they shall never languish again.
Then shall the young women rejoice in the dance,
    And the young men and the old shall be merry.
I will turn their mourning into joy,
    I will comfort them, and give them gladness for sorrow.
I will give the priests their fill of fatness,
    and my people shall be satisfied with my bounty,
                              says the Lord. (31:10, 12-14)

It is, however, the reenacted covenant that is Jeremiah's signature anticipation (31:31-34). It is acknowledged by the prophet that the older covenant has been broken. YHWH is resolved to make a new covenant, so that
the process of covenant broken and remade replicates the drama of Exodus
32–34. The new covenant, derived from Deuteronomy, will be Torah-based,
yielding an obedience that permits the reiteration of the covenant formula:
"I will put my law within them, and I will write it on their hearts; and I
will be their God, and they shall be my people" (v. 33). All of that "impossible impossibility" is grounded in YHWH's readiness to forgive and forget:
"I will forget their iniquity, and remember their sin no more" (v. 34). In
this vision of restoration, there is no mention of king or temple or city.
Rather Israel is taken back, yet again, to Sinai, so that we may hear echoes
of the contemporeneity of Moses in the on-going work of the Torah: "Not
with our ancestors did the Lord make this covenant, but with us, who are
all of us here alive today" (Deut. 5:3). The reiteration and reenactment of
covenant in Deuteronomy is followed in that chapter by the reiteration of
the decalogue (Deut. 5:6-17). Thus divine forgiveness is an act designed to
permit and empower new obedience.

That assertion of newness as new covenant would seem to be at the core
of Jeremianic hope. That hope, however, is fully grounded, in the final form
of the text, in appeals to creation theology, so that the reasserted fidelity of
YHWH is as reliable as the reliability of the created order:

Thus says the Lord,
who gives the sun as light by day
and the fixed order of the moon and the stars for light by night,
who stirs up the sea so that its waves roar—
the Lord of hosts in his name:
If this fixed order were ever to cease
from my presence, says the Lord,

then also the offspring of Israel would cease
to be a nation before me forever.
Thus says the LORD:
If the heavens can be measured,
and the foundations of the earth below can be explored,
then I will reject all the offspring of Israel
because of all they have done, says the LORD. (Jer. 31:35-37)

In what must be derivative texts in Jeremiah, it is also asserted that the new resolve of YHWH includes the restoration of the Davidic governance (33:17-18, 21) and of the ministry of the Levites (33:21), a practice with which Jeremiah has close ties. Again we are able to see that the particular refraction of hope is through the prism of specific tradition and experience. But the outcome is the same from these different perspectives: all things are possible for God!

C. Hope in the book of *Isaiah* is clustered in Isaiah 40–55, chapters that are distinguished from but intrinsically related to the foregoing materials of judgment in the book. We have already seen that in 40:28-31, 49:15-18, and 50:2-3 this poetry answers and intends to resolve the grieving complaints of Israel. Now we are able to see that the entire corpus of Isaiah 40–55 intends to announce and enact a new wave of the future given by YHWH that will lead to a jubilant return to Jerusalem. Thus of the term "gospel" ("good tidings") is distinct usage in this poetry (40:9; 41:27; 52:7). The term refers to the good news announced to the despairing in Babylon that YHWH is back in play with a show of power and resolve that will nullify the fearful power of Babylon. The theological claim is that YHWH is stronger than the gods of Babylon (46). The historical claim is that Cyrus, the Persian, will end Babylonian hegemony and permit Israel to go home (44:28; 45:1).

Thus the poetry of Isaiah is in a new doxological idiom that celebrates the great victory of YHWH over the oppressors of Israel who have refused to show mercy toward Israel, mercy that YHWH always had intended (47:6). In the face of such despair, YHWH announces and will enact "a new thing" that will be congruent with the exodus (Exod. 43:18-19). As YHWH was shown to be stronger than the ancient Pharaoh, so YHWH will be stronger than the Babylonians.

It is worth noting that in this poetry, appeal is made precisely to the tradition of Abraham. Thus it is on the basis of Abraham and Sarah that Israel may hope for a *novum* from YHWH:

Look to the rock from which you were hewn,
and to the quarry from which you were dug.

> Look to Abraham your father
>> and to Sarah who bore you;
> for he was but one when I called him,
>> but I blessed him and made him many. (51:1-2)

More specifically, the "barren one" (Israel) is now to be fruitful, generating a future (54:1-3). Thus we return to the narrative of Genesis 18. As the birth of that ancient mother was impossible, so the restoration of Israel is an impossibility that is as sure as YHWH's resolve.

The culmination of this poetry is a great scenario of departure from Babylon and a joyous return to Jerusalem. The poet had, at the outset, announced a great homecoming on a new highway:

> In the wilderness prepare the way of the LORD,
>> make straight in the desert a highway for our God.
> Every valley shall be lifted up,
>> and every mountain and hill be made low;
> the uneven ground shall become level,
>> and the rough places a plain.
> Then the glory of the LORD shall be revealed,
>> and all peoples shall see it together,
>> for the mouth of the LORD has spoken. (40:3-5)

The procession homeward will be led by YHWH in YHWH's glory. And in 55:12-13, the anticipated procession is under way:

> For you shall go out in joy,
>> and be led back in peace;
> the mountains and the hills before you
>> shall burst into song,
>> and all the trees of the field shall clap their hands. (v. 12)

All of creation is overjoyed at the emancipation of Israel!

The promissory theme in Isaiah is not confined to chapters 40–55. At the beginning of the book, the poet anticipates that in time to come Jerusalem (Zion) will be the epicenter of international relations. (2:2-4). YHWH's Torah will be the teacher and guideline for all peoples; the outcome will be a passion for peaceableness that is in contrast to the conventional practices of war.

That scenario is matched, at the end of the book of Isaiah, by a vision of a new creation that will feature humane social practices and social relationships.

The enactment of new creation will eventuate in the abiding availability of YHWH and the reconciliation of all creation:

> For I am about to create new heavens
> > and a new earth;
> The former things shall not be remembered
> > or come to mind.
> But be glad and rejoice forever
> > in what I am creating;
> for I about to create Jerusalem as a joy,
> > and its people as a delight.
> . . . .
> Before they call I will answer,
> > while they are yet speaking I will hear.
> The wolf and the lamb shall feed together,
> > The lion shall eat straw like the ox;
> > > but the serpent—his food shall be dust!
> They shall not hurt or destroy
> > on all my holy mountain,
> > > > > > > says the LORD. (65:17-18, 24-25)

The future is all about Jerusalem!

The poetry of Isaiah is familiar to us because of Handel's *Messiah*. Indeed, it is so familiar to us that it is readily taken as reified project for the future. It is important to recognize, given such a regard for the text, that it is all utterance. It is all imagination. The possibility for the future lives on the lips of the poets who are "given words."

The poetic offer is a new world about to be given. We should not miss that the poetry of promise carries with it an implicit summons as well. Thus the "wait" of 40:31 is an active, engaged leaning into the future, a turn from the past of despair. More specifically, in chapters 51–52 we may notice three imperatives that repeat the verb of summons that compels Israel, on hearing the poetry, to act toward the future:

- In Isaiah 51:17 it is "rouse":

> Rouse yourself, rouse yourself!
> > Stand up, O Jerusalem,
> you who have drunk at the hand of the LORD
> > the cup of his wrath,

> who have drunk to the dregs
>> the bowl of staggering.

The usage suggests that Israel, in its displacement, has been drunk with suffering and despair. But that stupor has gone on long enough; it is time to sober up, to stand up, and to pay attention. The verb "rouse" means to wake up, to be on the alert. In its drunkenness Israel is urged to slough off its despair and to notice what is new, namely, a chance to become resituated in Jerusalem in freedom.

- In 52:1-2 the double imperative introduces a series of imperatives that call for action:

> Awake, awake,
>> put on our strength, O Zion!
> Put on your beautiful garments,
>> O Jerusalem, the holy city;
> for the uncircumcised and the unclean
>> shall enter you no more.
> Shake yourself from the dust, rise up,
>> O captive Jerusalem;
> loose the bonds from your neck,
>> O captive daughter Zion! (52:1-2)

The initial verb is the same as that of 51:17, even if translated differently. This double usage is followed by more imperatives:

> put on;
> clothe;
> shake;
> rise up;
> loose.

The poem is a call to action. The imagery is a combination of military strength (v. 1), liturgical preparation (v. 1), and ripping off signs of servitude. It is a call to receive, embrace, and to act in the freedom YHWH has asserted.

- In 52:11-12 the imagery is of a departure and a great procession home:

> Depart, depart, go out from there!
>   Touch no unclean thing;
> go out from the midst of it, purify yourselves,
>   you who carry the vessels of the LORD.
> For You shall not go out in haste,
>   and you shall not go in flight;
> for the LORD will go before you,
>   And the God of Israel will be your rear guard. (52:11-12)

The rhetoric proposes that Israel is a purified people, or even a priesthood, that carries the temple vessels back home. The summons is to go in the assurance that YHWH will be a protective presence behind and before. The usage of "in haste" contrasts this to the exodus when Israel left in haste. Now YHWH is so much in control that Israel may depart bondage at its convenience.

It is clear that the sacerdotal vision of Ezekiel, the Torah-based hope of Jeremiah, and the city vision of Isaiah rely on very different imagery. It is equally clear that for all their differences, the sum of prophetic hope is that God is about to enact an impossibility. It is that impossibility that is the substance of the gospel. These poets, in their imaginative utterances, construed an alternative world for their listeners. That alternative world is not "too hard." It is rather the substance of things hoped for, the conviction of things not seen (Heb. 11:1). The alternative to bondage is in imagination that is offered as God's own resolve, offered through imaginative human utterance.

VI

The performance of future-opening possibility is continued, of course, into the New Testament. When we are faithful to those texts, we are compelled to preach hope that the world judges impossible. It is clear that the seal of all such impossibility is the church's exclamation that "Christ is risen." That large claim, however, is given concreteness and specificity, first of all, in the stories the church tells about Jesus. Here I will consider the Gospel of Luke as one account of the swirl of "impossibilities" around Jesus.

- I have cited, in my initial comments, an "impossibility" in the verdict of Gabriel to Mary: "For nothing will be impossible with God" (Luke 1:37). That declaration is carried through Luke's gospel and on into his book of Acts:

- Mary's song about the world revolution around Jesus is rooted in Abraham:

> He has helped his servant Israel,
>   in remembrance of his mercy,
> according to the promise he made to our ancestors,
>   to Abraham and to his descendants forever. (Luke 1:54-55)

- In Luke 7:22, in response to John, Jesus enumerates the impossibilities he has performed: "Go and tell John what you have seen and heard: the blind receive their sight, the lame walk, the lepers are cleansed, the deaf hear, the dead are raised, the poor have good news brought to them" (Luke 7:22). It is instructive and often noted that the series of transformations listed move toward ever greater radicality, toward the resurrection of the dead that is topped only by good news for the poor—surely an impossibility!
- In Luke 13:10-17, Jesus heals a woman he recognizes as a bearer of the promise of Abraham: "And ought not this woman, a daughter of Abraham whom Satan bound for eighteen long years, be set free from this bondage on the sabbath day?" (v. 16).
- In Luke 16:19-31, it is the poor, despised man who is welcomed to the bosom of Abraham: "He looked up and saw Abraham far away with Lazarus by his side" (v. 23).
- In Luke 19:1-10, Jesus identifies the despised tax collector as an heir to Abraham: "Today salvation has come to this house, because he too is a son of Abraham" (v. 9).

And surely Jesus' parables are tales of the impossibility. Of the two most treasured among us, the "Good Samaritan" is a rejected other who cares for and pays for his assumed enemy. And in the "Prodigal Son," a welcome homecoming for a disobedient, shaming son is an astonishment. Both Jesus' actions and his narratives exhibit Jesus' refusal of the world of the possible and his capacity for God's impossibilities that make all things new. The parables anticipate the new regime; the narratives actualize that alternative world.

VII

Now among us with our jaded politics, our confused morality, and our unbearable economics, we are nearly driven to despair. It is not, moreover, easy to locate ground for any new possibility. But there is a yearning and a wonderment:

> Can peace come here?
> Can justice appear among us?
> Can abundance be our future?
> Can war end?
> Can jobs be generated?

And there, in the midst of the yearning and the wonderment, stands the preacher—not a politician or an economist or an international negotiator. The preacher is one with words given, words other than her own. The question among us is, What words have been given? Surely the words given are roughly the same words that are always given, words of new possibility. The preacher's words, like the embodied Word, refuse the confinements of modern rationality and dare to utter yet another word. That utterance is an assurance with a summons within it. It is a call for new behavior and new horizon, made utterable by the one who gives words and who inhabits the words entrusted to us. Preaching that is "conformed to this world" (Rom. 12:2) is in fact not worth the effort, because those words are available elsewhere.

The preacher is an agent of "Bursts of Newness." Here in Romans 4:17, I believe, is the ultimate seal of testimony to the God of impossibility: ". . . who gives life to the dead and calls into existence the things that do not exist."

Hans Heinrich Schmid has judged that (a) creatio ex nihilo, (b) justification by faith, and (c) resurrection of the dead are synonymous claims.[15] They all attest to the capacity of God for bodily *novi* in the world. There is more to it than utterance. But such newness is not given without utterance, words that "pluck up" and "pull down," that "build" and "plant" (Jer. 1:10).

CHAPTER 6

The Continuing Mandate

IN 1884 DENIS WORTMAN wrote a hymn. He was a pastor in the Reformed Church in America and subsequently became the president of New Brunswick Seminary, a school of the Reformed Church in America. For the centenary of the seminary, he wrote the hymn with these words:

> God of the prophets, bless the prophets' heirs,
> Elijah's mantel o'er Elisha cast.
> Each age for its own solemn tasks prepares:
> make each one nobler, stronger than the last.
>
> Anoint them prophets! Make their ears attend
> to your divinest speech; their hearts awake
> To human need; their lips make eloquent
> for righteousness that shall all evil break.
>
> Anoint them priests! Strong intercessors they
> for pardon, and for charity and peace!
> O might with them the world, though gone astray,
> pass into Christ's pure life of sacrifice.
>
> Make them apostles! Heralds of your cross,
> forth may they go to tell all realms your grace.
> Inspired of you, may they count all but loss,
> and stand at last with joy before your face.[1]

For the seminary, the hymn hoped and imagined that the school was educating students to be prophets, priests, and apostles in the church.

I

I begin with this hymn because in my church tradition, it has been sung at many ordinations of pastors to the ministry of word and sacrament. The four verses of the hymn identify three offices or functions in that ministry:

- The fourth verse is, "Make them apostles" in order to "tell all realms your grace."
- The third verse is "anoint them priests." This is a curious theme in a free Calvinist church tradition, my own tradition that has always been resistant to priests as mediators. The text says "strong intercessors they," with an allusion to "pardon" and "sacrifice." The verse reflects a sacramental view of ministry that hardly squares with the faith of that tradition.
- But my interest is in verses one and two. The prophets, in sequence before priests or apostles, get two verses, with the address to God, "God of the prophets," with a series of petitions:

  - that God should bless the prophets' heirs (that word in the original was "sons" before being made inclusive), with reference to "human need" and "righteousness that shall all evil break."
  - that God should "anoint them prophets" with an allusion to Elisha as the successor to Elijah, the gratuitous assumption that the older generation had been prophetic.

The reason I begin here is to imagine the church singing not only in anticipation of coming apostles and priests, but two verses in hope of coming prophets. I know full well, of course, that congregations will sing almost anything put in front of them, whether in a hymnal or on a screen, so that the singing of hope for the coming prophets might well be, on the part of the congregation, largely unwitting.

Nevertheless, the church does sing such words, surely with a modicum of intentionality. There is a tacit yearning in the church for the prophetic. And so the church sings about the prophetic with some vigor, in contexts of ordination with adoring attentiveness to the woman or man who has "run the course" and made good thus far. The church sings that way with hope, all the while, in practice, mostly resisting anything prophetic and really wanting no more than a status quo pastorate or priesthood, mostly wanting apostolic faith that "tells" but does not summon too much.

It is in that context of a *singing affirmation* side by side with a *practical reluctance or resistance* that frames the continuing mandate to prophetic ministry. Those who would be prophetic are situated exactly in that ecclesial ambiguity, an ambiguity very often felt among us quite personally as we at the same time intend to take the call seriously and yet cringe from it when we get down to it. But the singing does not stop!

I conclude these presentations with some summary reflection on a contemporary call to be prophetic and on the contemporary practice of the prophetic. No doubt the prophetic dimension of ministry as a vocation of the *double divine impossibility* is made difficult because of the social conformity of the church and the diminution of the gospel. At the turn of the twentieth century, we spoke of the "acids of modernity," not fully seeing that those "acids" that eroded the clams of faith were the consequence of the entire modern Cartesian program of thin rationality that has made the task of "impossibility" nearly impossible with its embarrassing notion of divine agency, that is, as we now say, "an interventionist God."

But while recognizing that contemporary reality, my burden is to insist that there are clear direct and important connections between the summons of the prophetic in contemporary practice and the ancient prophetic burden by those who linger as our models and antecedents. These ancients, to be sure, were not "handicapped" by our modern thin, positivistic rationality. We do not have that in common. What we do have in common, however, is *a totalizing ideology of exceptionalism* that precludes critique of our entitlements and self-regard. In that ancient world, the totalizing ideology of Israel centered on David and the temple. In the contemporary Western world, that totalizing ideology takes the form of "chosenness" of white Western superiority that guarantees privilege and precludes serious change. The defining reality is not simply an intellectual problem of rationality, as acute as that surely is, but it is the socioeconomic, political status quo as a twin of that rationality that looms as context and challenge. Every serious preacher knows that guardians of such privilege and entitlement who fend off divine "impossibility" are remarkably alert and vigilant in the congregation to fend off any imagined challenge.

Long before the fall of the Berlin Wall, a young East German evangelical pastor told me that every sermon he preached was a life-or-death challenge, because he knew that he was, every Sunday, under surveillance for any utterance that questioned the totalizing ideology of the regime. But then, it has occurred to me that in our democratic society of "free speech," the preacher who would be prophetic about God's impossibilities is, in like manner—though more softly—under the same surveillance. That surveillance is not, I believe, because there is intellectual resistance to an interventionist God but because the intellectual resistance serves as a cover against penetrating and exposing the totalizing ideology that remains unnamed and unacknowledged among us, but that functions to define and legitimate a special place in the world. The prophetic tradition persistently *reperforms both impossibilities of dismantling and restoration*; and the totalizing ideology can host neither *the impossibility of dismantling* nor *the impossibility of restoration*. As the hymn affirms, however, the mandate continues with prophets and sons of prophets and daughters of prophets, those who have not succumbed to any totalizing ideology who continue to struggle with the freedom of the God who will not be mocked, or contained, even in our best rationality or our best ideology. Now I reflect on the contemporaneity of that call to the prophetic.

II

In the foregoing, I have insisted that the prophetic is not, contrary to some conservative views, a matter of prediction. Nor is it, contrary to some liberal views, a nagging or a scolding or righteous indignation about social justice. It is, rather, a sustained effort to imagine the world as though YHWH were a real character and the defining agent in the life of the world. And though it is a bit schematic, I have proposed that prophetic utterance, in every circumstance, bears witness to the two defining impossibilities that God continues to perform in the face of a closed rationality or a resistant ideology.

1. I have pointed to a script for these two impossibilities in the prayer and oracle of Jeremiah 32 that build from the narrative concerning Jeremiah's purchase of the family farm (vv. 1-15) that in turn builds from the narrative of the birth announcement to Sarah and Abraham in Genesis 18. *The impossibility is that YHWH will dismantle the Jerusalem establishment* that is celebrated as unconditionally guaranteed. In the prophetic prayer, Jeremiah indicts Israel and then declares about the God for whom nothing is impossible: "Therefore you have made all these disasters come on them. See, the siege-ramps have been cast up against the city to take it, and the city, faced with sword, famine, and pestilence, has been given into the hands of the Chaldeans who are fighting against it. What you spoke has happened, as you yourself can see" (vv. 23-24). And in the corresponding divine oracle of the God for whom nothing is impossible, it is asserted in God's own utterance: "Therefore thus

says the LORD: I am going to give this city into the hands of Chaldeans and into the hand of King Nebuchadnezzar of Babylon, and he shall take it. The Chaldeans who are fighting against this city shall come, set it on fire, and burn it, with the houses on whose roofs offerings have been made to Baal and libations have been poured out to other gods, to provoke me to anger" (vv. 28-29). These utterances anticipate and enact YHWH's severity against an economic, political establishment that has unbearably become perverse.

Both the prophetic prayer and the divine oracle, however, go on to *a second impossibility,* because prophetic utterance does not end in judgment. In the prayer, the prophet concludes: "Yet you, O Lord GOD, have said to me, 'Buy the field for money and get witnesses'—though the city has been given into the hands of the Chaldeans" (v. 25). And in the oracle YHWH declares:

> See, I am going to gather them from all the lands to which I drove
> them in my anger and my wrath and in great indignation; I will bring
> them back to this place, and I will settle them in safety. They shall be
> my people, and I will be their God. I will give them one heart and one
> way, that they may fear me for all time, for their own good and the
> good of their children after them. I will make an everlasting covenant
> with them, never to draw back from doing good to them; and I will
> put the fear of me in their hearts that they may not turn from me. I
> will rejoice in doing good to them, and I will plant them in this land in
> faithfulness, with all my heart and all my soul. (vv. 37-41)

Both utterances of the second impossibility of restoration begin with *hinneh,* "Behold" (vv. 24, 37). Pay attention! It is a surprise. No one in conventional ideology would have guessed that a second impossibility would follow after the first harsh one. Prophetic discourse is a watch for God's goodness beyond deathliness.

2. The point is more programmatic at the outset of Jeremiah's prophetic call. After Jeremiah is called by YHWH and he resists the call, YHWH then gives the mandate that will be enacted in the book that follows:

> See, today I appoint you over nations and over kingdoms,
>   to pluck up and to pull down,
> to destroy and to overthrow,
>   to build and to plant. (1:10)

The prophet is designated for two tasks. *The first task* is "to pluck up and to pull down, to destroy and to overthrow." These four verbs recur in the tradition that follows, but it is the first two that define the task, "pluck up and pull down." Jeremiah's mandate is to deconstruct the totalizing ideology of Jerusalem and to utter its dismantling.

The second part of the mandate yields the second impossibility, "to plant and to build." Thus "plant" counters "pluck up" and "build" counters "pull down." The prophet is to terminate what has been established. Note well, the prophet is not mandated to talk about what God will do but is to "do" it by utterance. It is the utterance that the socially constructed world of exceptionalism has been put forward. Now it is by utterance that it is to be exposed and terminated. It is by utterance, moreover, that a restored social arrangement, beyond the totalizing impetus, is to be reconstrued and made available. It is by utterance!

3. The point of *the double prophetic assignment* of enacting *the double impossibility* is summarized later in the Jeremiah tradition in the context of hope-filled oracles: "Just as I have watched over them to pluck up and break down, to overthrow, destroy, and bring evil, so I will watch over them to build and to plant, says the LORD" (31:28). The same verbs are reiterated, only now there is a fifth verb added to the acts of rejection, "Pluck up, break down, destroy, overthrow, and *bring evil*." And there are the same two positives, "build and plant." In this verse, the two enactments of impossibility are given in sequence: "just as . . . so . . . ." The utterance is *after* the dismantling and *before* the restoration, given loss, awaiting new gift.

4. The prophetic materials in Jeremiah 32, 1:10, and 31:18 voice the historical experience and historical hope of Jerusalem. The fact on the ground is that there was a "tearing down" and a "plucking up." There was a destruction, a deportation, and a disruption of the coveted ideology of exceptionalism. That deep wound to Jerusalem, so well lined out in the book of Lamentations, shows that the event matches the word. The second fact on the ground is that there was a restoration and a rebuilding of the city, with reference to Haggai and Zechariah and then Ezra and Nehemiah, and some would say a continuation of rebuilding in the contemporary state of Israel. Thus the history of the city is read, in textual imagination, as a process of exile and return. The exile was an impossibility that occurred; the restoration was an impossibility that occurred. Prophetic utterance mapped out the truth of Israel's life in the world.

5. In Christian tradition, that divine impossibility of exile and restoration is transposed in the life of Jesus and reperformed in his body. The dismantling of Jerusalem is reenacted in the *crucifixion of Jesus*. It is clear in the tradition that the death of the Messiah was an impossibility. So Peter: "God forbid it, Lord! This must never happen to you" (Matt. 16:22). The death of the Messiah could not happen! It is clear, moreover, that the dismantling of

Jerusalem is now taken as a trope for the crucifixion of Jesus, for the Fourth Gospel witnesses: "Jesus answered them, 'Destroy this temple, and in three days I will raise it up.' The Jews then said, 'This temple has been under construction for forty-six years, and will you raise it up in three days?' But he was speaking of the temple of his body" (John 2:19-21). It is equally clear that the *resurrection of Jesus* is a reenactment of the restoration of Jerusalem and is surely a second impossibility.[2] In New Testament articulation, the double impossibility of *crucifixion and resurrection* are both acts of God that defy the reason of this age. Both impossibilities, moreover, rooted in the prophetic crucible of the Old Testament: "For I handed on to you as of first importance what I in turn had received; that *Christ died* for our sins in accordance with the scriptures, and that he was buried, and that *he was raised* on the third day in accordance with the scriptures" (1 Cor. 15:3-4). The recital appeals to the prophetic script. This model of crucifixion and resurrection—with the deep abyss of Saturday between—has been stunningly lined out by Alan Lewis in his meditation on Saturday.[3] His exposition carries the force of this model into world history in contemporary society as he takes up in turn Auschwitz, Hiroshima, and Chernobyl, each surely an impossibility, each creating a dread-filled chasm that awaits Easter reconstruction.

6. These twinned impossibilities of crucifixion and resurrection are given dramatic sacramental force in the performance of baptism. Moving from the model of *exile-restoration* to the more radical model of *crucifixion-resurrection*, baptism is the *reperformance of Friday and Sunday:* "Therefore we have been buried with him by *baptism into death,* so that, just as Christ was *raised from the dead* by the glory of the Father, so we too might walk in newness of life" (Rom. 6:4). The descent into the waters is indeed to be buried with him, to die to the old life. The emergence from these with a new identity, "sealed as Christ's own forever," is a second impossibility that empowers "newness of life." When baptism is taken with sacramental seriousness, it is the performance of *twinned evangelical impossibilities,* of losing the old life and receiving the new life; thus the baptized do indeed replicate and reiterate the *Jewish drama of exile and restoration* and the *Christological drama of Friday and Sunday.*

7. And now, as we bid the "God of the prophets" to anoint the prophetic heirs, we take this double impossibility of "plucking up and pulling down, of planting and building," of exile and restoration, of crucifixion and resurrection, of dying with Christ and being raised with him to new life, and we ponder our contemporary prophetic mandate as we in our turn are called to enact that double impossibility.

Our context, so it seems to me, is ripe for such a ministry. It is ripe because as anyone can see who looks, the impossibility of dismantling is under way in our society, in Western culture, and in the world generally. The old "business as usual" cannot any longer be credibly sustained.

Everyone can trace moreover, the emerging impossibility of restoration in new modes, new power arrangements, and new formulations of truth that have important discontinuity from what has gone before. I propose that in all the ways that are politically bearable and rhetorically imaginable, the prophetic-pastoral ministry is to walk with people in and through these two impossibilities. I believe, moreover, that it is only a faith community that is in deep touch with this daring rhetorical tradition that can perform this indispensible pastoral act.

III

The first task of contemporary prophetic ministry is to empower and enable folk to *relinquish* a world that is passing from us.

1. *The ancient task of relinquishment* was to face the reality that the Jerusalem establishment, king and temple, no longer enjoyed unconditional guarantees and immunity from the vagaries of history. The prophets voice this impossibility:

- In a daring public drama Hosea names his children with stunning names, "Not Pitied," "Not My People": "Then the Lord said, 'Name her Lo-ruhamah, for I will no longer have pity on the house of Israel or forgive them.' . . . When she had weaned Lo-ruhamah, she conceived and bore a son. Then the Lord said, 'Name him Lo-ammi, for you are not my people and I am not your God'" (Hos. 1:6, 8).

The second impossibility follows for Hosea:

> I will have pity on Lo-ruhamah,
>   And I will say to Lo-ammi,
> "You are my people";
>   and he will say, "You are my God." (Hos. 2:23)

- In his rumination on his visit to the potter's house, Jeremiah can have God declare:

> So will I break this people and this city, as one breaks a pot-
> ter's vessel, so that it can never be mended. (Jer. 19:11)

Never mended! Never healed! Beyond repair!

- Eventually, even YHWH must admit that there has been a divine
  abandonment: "For a brief moment I abandoned you. . . . In
  overflowing wrath for a moment I hid my face from you . . ." (Isa.
  54:7-8). The abandonment has been momentary; in that moment,
  however, it has been complete. The impossible has happened.
  God has forsaken God's own people. That people, address in this
  poetic admission, must come to terms with the impossible loss.

2. In our time, the dismantling is surely epitomized by 9/11, for that
attack, minimal in actual scale, makes visible the loss of invulnerability, the
loss of guaranteed entitlement. The impossibility of an attack upon us in the
United States, with the coming loss of hegemony in the world, with the loss
of assumed white superiority, and with the noticeable ineffectiveness of our
military apparatus to accomplish is goals—all of that is happening to us, with
a general awareness of the unraveling.

3. Such costly relinquishment inevitably evokes *denial*, the pretence that it
is not happening and that it need not happen, that greater resolve will halt the
demise that better leadership can reverse the pattern, or that God will soon
reverse course, because it cannot happen here.

In that ancient world of Israel, Hananiah is the great icon of denial. In Jeremiah 27, the prophet speaks of the "yoke" of Babylon, soon to be imposed on
Judah, that is, the work of YHWH: "Bring your necks under the yoke of the
king of Babylon, and serve him and his people, and live. Why should you and
your people die by the sword, by famine, and by pestilence, as the LORD has
spoken concerning any nation that will not serve the king of Babylon? Do not
listen to the words of the prophets who are telling you not to serve the king of
Babylon, for they are prophesying a lie to you" (vv. 12-14). Jeremiah anticipated
that guaranteed Jerusalem would soon come under the military, political control of Nebuchadnezzar. But Hananiah countered that prophetic impossibility
with an assurance derived from the old conviction of chosenness: "Within two
years I will bring back to this place all the vessels of the LORD's house, which
King Nebuchadnezzar of Babylon took away from this place and carried to
Babylon. I will also bring back to this place King Jeconiah son of Jehoiakim of
Judah, and all the exiles from Judah who went to Babylon, says the LORD, for
I will break the yoke of the king of Babylon" (28:3-4).

The two prophets with their very different perspectives argue in public. Jeremiah wishes that Hananiah were telling the truth (28:6). But he knows better (vv. 7-10)!

In our own time, the denial of what must be relinquished among us is everywhere around us. The political mantra "Take back our country" is a desperate yearning not just for small government but for a safe, white, straight world from which the disruptive "others"—gays, Muslims, immigrants—are banished. That denial is featured in the seventh-inning stretch of professional baseball games where we sing, according to the mantra of military consumerism, "God bless America," God reinvigorate exceptionalism, God give us back the old world. The practice of such unreflective crowd action must have been anticipated in the Songs of Zion that were sung defiantly or unknowingly in the Jerusalem temple even as the Babylonian army marched toward the city:

> God is our refuge and strength,
> a very present help in trouble.
> . . . .
> There is a river whose streams make glad the city of God,
> the holy habitation of the Most High.
> God is in the midst of the city; it shall not be moved . . . (Ps. 46:1, 4-5)

There is a deep current of denial among us, a wish-world that the ancient guarantees of the kind we prefer is on offer. But it is a lie, because the surge of history (that we say is God-governed) is inexorable. Thus the first task of the prophet is to process the relinquishment of what is treasured being taken from us.[4]

IV

The second task of contemporary prophetic ministry is to enable and empower folk to receive a new world that is emerging before our very eyes that we confess to be a gift of God.

1. *The ancient task of reception* was to face the emerging reality of a new Jerusalem. This new Jerusalem is lined out in lyrical fashion by Isaiah:

> But be glad and rejoice forever
> in what I am creating;
> for I am about to create Jerusalem as a joy,

and its people as a delight.
I will rejoice in Jerusalem,
    and delight in my people;
no more shall the sound of weeping be heard in it,
    or the cry of distress.
No more shall there be in it
    an infant that lives but a few days,
    or an old person who does not live out a lifetime;
for one who dies at a hundred years will be considered a youth,
    and one who falls short of a hundred will be considered accursed.
They shall build houses and inhabit them;
    they shall plant vineyards and eat their fruit.
They shall not build and another inhabit;
    they shall not plant and another eat . . . (Isa. 65:18-22)

That is the lyric!

But in fact the restored city on the ground was not so grand. The modest rebuilding in the time of Haggai and Zechariah and the more formidable reconstruction under Ezra and Nehemiah was not very impressive. Indeed the new reality required a redefinition and a recharacterization of Judaism as a "culture of interpretation" in Jerusalem that, perforce, modest in its worldly ambition.[5] The new world of restored Jerusalem was not to be a "royal kingdom" but a tax-paying colony of the Persian Empire.

Isaiah can dare to identify Cyrus the Persian conqueror as the Messiah of YHWH, thus a rescue by a Gentile (Isa. 45:1). How embarrassing that the rescue would not even be a Jewish rescue, as though Jews were no longer players on the geo-political scene. Now in their vulnerable weakness, Jews could only receive what is given on terms other than their own. We are able to see, in Isaiah 45:9-13, that there was deep resistance among Jews in exile to the proposed rescue by a Gentile that Isaiah had announced. They must have questioned the divine offer of a new world to be lived on Persian terms. The poet chides Israel for doubting, quarreling, and resisting YHWH's intention:

Woe to you who strive with your Maker,
    earthen vessels with the potter!
Does the clay say to the one who fashions it, "What are you
    making"?
    or "Your work has no handles"?
Woe to anyone who says to a father, "What are you begetting?"

or to a woman, "With what are you in labor?"
Thus says the LORD,
    The Holy One of Israel, and its Maker:
Will you question me about my children,
    or command me concerning the work of my hands?
I made the earth,
    and created humankind upon it;
it was my hands that stretched out the heavens,
    and I commanded all their host.
I have aroused Cyrus in righteousness,
    and I will make all his paths straight;
he shall build my city
    and set my exiles free,
not for price or reward,
    says the LORD of hosts. (vv. 9-13)

The first image is of clay challenging the potter. The second image is of sperm questioning the father, or an embryo questioning the mother in labor. No, clay does not question the potter. No, sperm does not question the father. No, the embryo does not question the mother. No, Israel does not question or resist YHWH. The new world will be given as God gives it, whether Israel likes it or not.

- Ezra can bemoan the economic political reality of the new world of Persian hegemony. His pathos-filled prayer ends with a grief filled petition: "Here we are, *slaves to this day*—slaves in the land that you gave to our ancestors to enjoy its fruit and its good gifts. Its rich yield goes to the kings whom you have set over us because of our sins; they have power also over our bodies and over our livestock at their pleasure, and we are in great distress" (Neh. 9:36-37). As a Persian agent, Ezra must have been enthused about the restoration of Jerusalem. But then it dawned on him and the elite managers financed by Persia: It is all about Persia! It is all about Persian taxes! It is all about the world not being as we Jews had imagined it. It is all about the distress of receiving a world on terms other than our own, even if the Persian arrangement is taken, via Isaiah as YHWH's gift and initiative.
- In the early days of Persian rebuilding, Zechariah recognized that it is "the day of small things" (Zech. 4:10). The great lyric of

Isaiah did not come to fruition. The restoration was not glorious. But it is what was given and is here acknowledged.

2. The second impossibility in contemporary prophetic ministry is *the reception of the new world* that is being given to us by the mercy of God. It is not the old grand world de jevu. It is other than that, and from the perspective of that old world, it is less than it was. So consider, in the face of failed exceptionalism:

- No doubt a lowered standard of living;
- Perhaps water rationing before very long, not to mention oil costs and shortages;
- The loss of military dominance and political hegemony in the world, even if we seek a next government that employs swash-buckling rhetoric;
- Most of all, it is a new world where "the other" looms large and is experienced by many as a threat. Dominant culture has given up, after a struggle, keeping Blacks "in their place" and keeping women in the kitchen. That dominant culture still has hopes, however, of keeping gays in the closet and keeping immigrants out away from the borders, and keeping Muslims away from urban mosques. And now the "other" looms large among us, no longer hidden, and so disruptive of the homogeneity of a world under our comfortable control.

This is not, on my part, an "advocacy" for a social reality peopled by "others." It is, rather, to recognize that a "rainbow coalition" is not finally an invention of Jesse Jackson; it is a coalition that will be indispensible in order to forge and sustain a viable public infrastructure. The recognition of that world is a huge, demanding enterprise that requires immense pastoral imagination. Indeed, given old ideological maps, the acceptance of such a culture of "the other" is an impossibility, but now an impossibility given to us that will not go away. That social impossibility, of course, is not unlike the crisis faced by Paul among Gentiles in the early church.

3. It is no surprise that such a second impossibility—the reception of a new world—ancient or contemporary, evokes *despair* rather than welcome. The despair in that ancient world is voiced in Lamentations:

He has made my teeth grind on gravel,
    and made me cower in ashes;
my soul is bereft of peace;

> I have forgotten what happiness is;
> so I say, "Gone is my glory,
>   and all that I had hoped for from the LORD."
> The thought of my affliction and my homelessness
>   is wormwood and gall!
> My soul continually thinks of it
>   and is bowed down within me. (Lam. 3:16-20)

The new world does indeed make our teeth grind if we endlessly cherish and lust for what is old and gone. It is worth noting that the next verses of the poem recover hope through memories of YHWH's fidelity:

> But this I call to mind,
>   and therefore I have hope:
> The steadfast love of the Lord never ceases,
>   his mercies never come to an end;
> they are new every morning;
>   great is your faithfulness.
> "The Lord is my portion," says my soul,
>   "therefore I will hope in him." (Lam. 3:21-24)

Such recovery and buoyancy, however, comes to reality only later. For now, there is lost hope.

In our time the despair is because that old treasured world is gone, efforts at salvage and restoration are futile, and the public process is "out of control." It is too soon, for most folk, to receive a theological verdict that "God has revoked American exceptionalism." We are, however, close to that if and when we acknowledge that there is no going back. It is the same acknowledgement that finally was required in Jerusalem. Those who rebuilt that ancient city were required to fashion a very different notion of exceptionalism; no doubt that same work stands in front of our society.

V

Thus I reach a formulation of the twin impossibilities of prophetic awareness:

1. There is (God-given) *loss* that actualizes the "woe" of being out of sync with God's purposes that require relinquishment. That relinquishment in turn produces *denial*. Thus:

> Loss, relinquishment, denial.

2. There is a (God-given) *new emergent* that actualizes "the days are coming" by the wise generativity of God that requires receptivity. That receptivity in turn evokes *despair.* Thus:

> New emergent, receptivity, despair.

Prophetic preaching, I propose, is situated exactly at the epicenter of these two impossibilities, an occasion signed as "Saturday" by Alan Lewis. Prophetic preaching is situated in the midst of:

> Relinquishment and denial,
> Reception and despair.

The work that is to be done prophetically is not a discussion or advocacy concerning "issues," though "issues" must be faced. The pastoral-prophetic task is deeply beneath specific issues; it concerns a substructure of a "felt world" that is variously known as threat or opportunity, as gift or wound. I believe that prophetic ministry that swirls around *truth* (*against denial*) and *hope* (*against despair*) is undertaken not because of moral passion (though that counts) but because without the prophetic processing of denial and despair, our society will devour itself in alienation.

VI

The prophetic task occurs amid a denying, despairing, totalizing ideology that is willfully set against the inscrutable holiness of God. That totalizing control, with its wealth, power, technology, and propaganda, presents itself as the only game in town with nothing outside its domain. This is what makes it "total." That is what evokes "totalizing" practice. That is what runs toward the "totalitarian." In the face of that unnamed, unacknowledged powerful reality come the prophets who have words of *truth-telling* and *hope-summoning.* It is an unequal contest because "Jerusalem," metaphor for all totalizing ideologies, is not hospitable to the prophets. Thus Jesus: "Yet today, tomorrow, and the next day I must be on my way because it impossible for a prophet to be killed outside of Jerusalem. Jerusalem, Jerusalem, the city that kills the prophets and stones those who are sent to it! How often have I desired to gather your children together as a hen gathers her brood under her wings, and you were not willing!" (Luke 13:33-34). What the biblical tradition knows, however, is that true speech has transformative power and is not finally silenced.[6] So the tradition attests, right down to Havel and King and Berrigan and Tutu and Lerner and Wallis. My sense about *the God-given word* vis-á-vis *totalizing ideology* is illuminated by three readings I mention here.

1. Emmanuel Levinas, in his great book, *Infinity and Totality*, articulates reality through the ethical engagement with the face of the other.[7] That is, the truth is not found in system or in formulation but in the actual *human face of the other.* From this defining insight, the title of his book bears much fruit. By "totality," Levinas means a closely contained system, whether political, economic, moral, social, theological, or whatever. By "infinity," he means, as an alternative, an openness to what is new and possible and given that is not limited by present power arrangements or theological restraints. It is easy enough, and obvious, to locate contemporary Western hegemony under the rubric of "totality." What interests us, however, is our capacity to locate prophetic preaching under the rubric of "infinity," of open possibility that defies containment. It is for that reason that the ancient poets could engage in daring scandalous rhetoric in order to think the unthinkable and to say the unsayable.[8] For it is the *unthinkable* and the *unsayable* that bear witness to *divine impossibility.*

2. Martha Nussbaum has offered a tour de force in her book, *The Clash Within.*[9] It is a study of the Hindu-Muslim conflict in India. Nussbaum discerns that the real conflict is not between Hindus and Muslims, as much as our usual presentations say so. It is, rather, a clash between those open to the other and those resistant to the other:

> The clash between proponents of ethnoreligious homogeneity and proponents of a more inclusive and pluralistic type of citizenship is a clash between two types of people within a single society. At the same time, this clash exposes tendencies that are present, at some level, within most human beings: the tendency to seek domination as a form of self-protection, versus the ability to respect others who are different, and to see in difference a nation's richness rather than a threat to its purity.[10]

Her title, *The Clash Within*, is designed to be an answer to and refutation of Samuel Huntington's thesis in *The Coming Clash of Civilizations*, in which he anticipates that the Christian West and Islam are on an inescapable collision course with each other.[11] Against that, Nussbaum, in a hypothesis of which I am fully persuaded, proposes that the "real clash" is not between civilizations but within two "types of people." Her powerful conclusion is this: "The real 'clash of civilizations' is not 'out there,' between admirable Westerners and Muslim zealots. It is here, within each person, as we oscillate uneasily between self-protective aggression and the ability to live in the world with others."[12]

I believe that her defining insight in this study is of paramount importance for the practice of prophetic impossibility. The world that is being reshaped and relinquished among us is that of a homogenous, white, male-dominated, straight society. The world that is emerging before us is a world peopled by others who do not fit that neat, reassuring arrangement. The prophetic task, in light of Nussbaum's study, is to mediate *a relinquishment of a world that is gone* and *a reception of a world that is being given.* It is not so difficult to imagine that that old world is "being judged" for its violent exclusivism. Insofar as the "clash" is within, it becomes the pastoral-prophetic opportunity to process that clash and to legitimate the proper reality of the other as gift from God. This is in keeping, of course, with the ancient Torah commandments concerning the neighbor, a trajectory extended, for example, in Isaiah 58 to others so unlike "us."

3. Lawrence Thornton has written a novel entitled *Imagining Argentina*.[13] Thornton's story concerns Carlos, an Argentinean in the midst of a repressive regime of disappearing persons. Carlos is preoccupied with the recovery of persons seized by the military state. Carlos's primary accent is to refuse to accept the "given world" in front of him and to imagine otherwise in a way that opens opportunities for happenings that the regime had declared impossible. On the one hand, Carlos speaks of "the generals in the car," the anonymous, faceless, ominous agents of the torturing regime, a cadre represented in the story by General Guzman. He is a perfect embodiment of a totalizing ideology. Of him (and those whom he represents) Carlos can say: "They can see everything they want to, but never forget that they cannot see beyond the distortion of their imagination where there is no color and everything exists in black and white."[14] In direct address to Guzman, Carlos asserts:

> One day, General, you will remember this conversation, not for what I have said up to now, but for this: Your belief would reduce us in size, shrink us to the little heads the forest people used once for barter and symbols. They were primitive and so it is easy to understand their desires. You are not. You believe that cutting off our heads and then shrinking them will stop us, that the knowledge of your willingness to do it will frighten everyone. You believe you can kill us. That is what you will remember, that you made the terrible mistake of not knowing what to kill. The danger to you is invisible and perhaps you will never understand it.[15]

As he draws his conclusions about the attitude and conduct of Carlos, Thom-ton makes this comment on behalf of Carlos.

> To see inside Guzman's mind at that moment would have revealed nothing but dust and mirages, the shape of an idea like that given a cone of wind in the pampas by the dust it sucks from the ground. He could never comprehend that my stories are more dangerous to him than the Mannlicher, my words more explosive than bombs planted in the Casa Rosada. That was what stopped me, why I let him live, for the bullet would have sent me into exile and silence. If, in return, he chooses to cut out my tongue I can write. If he smashes my hands, I can draw pictures in the dust with a stick held between my teeth. His life is a puny exchange for such power.[16]

Carlos does not accept or salute the fantasy world produced and sustained by the regime. He imagines outside "the given" with a force that is emancipatory and subversive:

> So long as we accept what the men in the car imagine, we're fin-ished. . . . We have to believe in the power of imagination because it is all we have, and ours is stronger than theirs.[17] And that is why we will survive, because they do not have what is necessary to defeat us. The real war is between imagination and theirs, what we can see and what they are blind to. Do not despair. None of them can see far enough, and so long as we do not let them violate our imagination we will survive.[18]

I have learned from Thornton (what Cavanaugh has found appropriate to the church in Chile under the regime of Pinochet) that "establishment imagination" is finally a claim without authority or power. Conversely, the emancipatory imagination of the prophets (à la Carlos) is wild, transformative, and restorative.

Thus I propose that prophetic utterance is the daring rhetorical practice of impossibility that appeals to the character of YHWH as the defining agent in the life of the world. This act of imagination knows and trusts that the world is open and supple and that every attempt to freeze it into absolute certitude or into unchanging power arrangements is an illusion. It is an illusion because the world is creaturely and it lives with reference to the will of the creator who gives and who withholds life (Deut. 32:39; Isa. 45:7).

The context for such suppleness in the imagination of Israel is the practice of the Psalms that always move back and forth between *lament–complaint–protest* and *praise–thanks*. In its speech before YHWH, Israel is always giving voice to its *loss* (*without denial*) and to its *hope* (*without despair*). That wide and deep rhetorical practice in Israel is epitomized in the drama of Psalm 30 wherein the story is told of the movement from solidity (v. 6) to dismantling loss (v. 7), to petition (v. 8-10), and finally to glad restoration (vv. 11-12). This psalm, a model for Israel, traces the drama from the first impossibility of dismaying loss to the second impossibility of wondrous grace. Or as the psalmist puts it succinctly:

> For his anger is but for a moment;
>   his favor is for a lifetime.
> Weeping may linger for the night,
>   but joy comes in the morning. (v. 5)

Israel does not deny the weeping of loss that lasts all night. Israel also does not lose heart about the newness that comes in the morning with joy.

VII

Finally, a sobering coda. I have laid out, as best I could, the great vocation of prophetic preaching with all the clarity that I can muster. Any reader of my words who may live and work in a local congregation will notice the enormous distance between this model and the real-life practice of the congregation. I am aware of this distance and am under no illusion about what a pastor in a local congregation may do as a prophetic preacher. I know very well that the local congregation itself is often to some extent a venue for totalizing ideology. I know very well, moreover, that we as pastors are, willingly or not, participants in that totalizing ideology. This book is not a scold or a reprimand to pastors about these matters, nor is it a call to heroic action in the congregation. I have a more modest intent—one that I believe is crucial for the health and faithfulness of our common ministry. It is this: the preacher must, in my judgment, in the midst of our current cultural upheaval, pay close attention to what is entrusted to the church and specifically to its ministers. The local congregation continues to be a matrix for *emancipatory, subversive utterance* that is not amenable to *totalizing ideology*. People continue to come to church to hear the wonder of Scripture and to respond, "The word of the Lord . . . thanks be to God." People continue to sit and listen attentively to the exposition of the word. People still entertain the odd thought, in spite of the reductionisms of modernity, that God is a real character and the defining agent in the life of the world. People still gather in church to hear and struggle with what is not on offer anywhere else.

Thus in taking a deep breath, preachers might take note that the local congregation is most likely the only place in town to host in serious ways the impossibilities of loss and newness that are the truth of our life with God. Indeed, the logic of Paul affirms: "But how are they to call on one in whom they have not believed? And how are they to believe in one of whom they have never heard? And how are they to hear without someone to proclaim him? And how are they to proclaim him unless they are sent?" (Rom. 10:14-15). The sequence of "send, proclaim, hear, believe" is the Pauline calculus that culminates with "beautiful feet." The reference is to Isaiah 52:7, with the "beautiful feet" bringing the new world of peace and salvation to a waiting community in crisis. The substance of the message carried by the feet is,

> Your God reigns.

That is the substance of the gospel, and it is all gospel in Isaiah 52:7 (see Mark 1:14-15). That formula, "Your God reigns," breaks out beyond the totalizing ideology of Babylon and beyond the despair of Israel and makes new possibility available.

The new impossibility is that Israel is now able to depart Babylon and its paralyzing claims.[19] Thus in the lyrical articulation at the end of Second Isaiah:

> For you shall go out in joy,
>   and be led back in peace;
> the mountains and the hills before you
>   shall burst into song,
>   and all the trees of the field shall clap their hands. (55:12)

Israel is always leaving Babylon. Israel is always leaving Egypt. What Michael Walzer says of Egypt is true of Babylon: "First, that wherever you live, it is probably Egypt; second, that there is a better place, a world more attractive, a promised land; and third, that 'the way to the land is through the wilderness.' There is no way to get from here to there except by joining together and marching."[20] God's people are always departing the lethal grip of the ordinarily possible. The departure depends upon utterance to exhibit as possible what the empire has long judged to be impossible.

But in the end, we are sober. In Mark 6:30-44 and 8:1-10, it is written that Jesus performed impossibilities of abundance—twice! He fed five thousand

and had twelve baskets of bread as surplus, and he fed four thousand and had seven baskets of bread as abundance. He did that twice. But Mark adds laconically about the disciples:

> They did not understand about the loaves, because their hearts were hardened. (Mark 6:52)

The disciples had no clue about the impossibility that Jesus had performed as a world of abundance. And the reason they failed to understand the impossibility is that they had hard hearts. That is, they still thought in terms of scarcity like pharaoh, the one with a hard heart (see Exodus 9:12; 10:10, 27; 11:10; 14:4). They still perceived the world through a totalizing ideology. They missed all the action!

We do not readily depart such an ideology. Neither people in church nor pastors depart easily. We do, nonetheless, yearn and trust for more than the empire can offer. We yearn for abundance and transformation and restoration. We yearn beyond the possible. That impossible is given, when it is given, on the quivering lips of the poet who refuses the thin offer of the totalizers.

NOTES

1. The Narrative Embedment of Prophetic Preaching

1. Joseph Blenkinsopp, *A History of Prophecy in Israel*, rev. ed. (Louisville: Westminster John Knox, 1996); Ronald E. Clements, *Old Testament Prophecy: From Oracles to Canon* (Louisville: Westminster John Knox, 1996); Klaus Koch, *The Prophets: The Assyrian Period* (Philadelphia: Fortress Press, 1983); Klaus Koch *The Prophets: The Babylonian and Persian Periods* (Philadelphia: Fortress Press, 1984); D. N. Premnath, *Eighth Century Prophets: A Social Analysis* (St. Louis: Chalice, 2003); Robert R. Wilson, *Prophecy and Society in Ancient Israel* (Philadelphia: Fortress Press, 1980).

2. On the ecclesial practicalities of prophetic preaching, see Leonora Tubbs Tisdale, *Prophetic Preaching: A Pastoral Approach* (Louisville: Westminster John Knox, 2010).

3. See Walter Brueggemann, "Four Proclamatory Confrontations in Scribal Refraction," *SJT* 56, no. 4 (2003): 404–26.

4. See Walter Brueggemann, *The Prophetic Imagination*, 2nd ed. (Minneapolis: Fortress Press, 2001).

5. On prophetic movement beyond a call to repent, see A. Vanlier Hunter, *Seek the Lord! A Study of the Meaning and Function of the Exhortations in Amos, Hosea, Isaiah, Micah, and Zephaniah* (Baltimore: St. Mary's Seminary and University, 1982).

6. See Pablo Richard, et al., *The Idols of Death and the God of Life: A Theology* (Maryknoll: Orbis, 1983).

7. Thus it is not very difficult to see that Richard Dawkins and Christopher Hitchens have made an idol of science by their absolutist claims that allow for no critique.

8. See the compelling discussion of Terry Eagleton, *Reason, Faith, and Revolution: Reflections on the God Debate* (New Haven: Yale University Press, 2009).

9. The material pay-out of this contest is offered in the narrative of Naboth's vineyard in 1 Kings 21 where a contest between economic theories of land is at play.

10. Walter Brueggemann, "Counterscript: Living with the Elusive God," *Christian Century* 122, no. 24 (November 29, 2005): 22–28.

11. Bruce Feiler, *America's Prophet: Moses and the American Story* (New York: William Morrow, 2009) has traced the way in which biblical rhetoric is intertwined with political claims in the United States.

12. On US exceptionalism, see Gary Dorrien, "Consolidating the Empire: Neoconservatism and the Politics of American Dominion," *Political Theology* 6, no. 4 (2005): 409–28, and John Updike, et al, "The Future of an American Idea," *The Atlantic* (November 2007): 13–62.

13. Gerhard von Rad, *The Problem of the Hexateuch and Other Essays* (New York: McGraw-Hill, 1966), 1–78.

14. C. H. Dodd, *The Apostolic Preaching and Its Developments* (New York: Harper and Brothers, n.d.).

15. Ibid., 3.

16. Franz Rosenzweig, *The Star of Redemption* (Notre Dame: University of Notre Dame, 1985), 93–261.

17. See Richard A. Horsley, *Jesus and Empire: The Kingdom of God and the New World Disorder* (Minneapolis: Fortress Press, 2003); Neil Elliott, *The Arrogance of Nations: Reading Romans in the Shadow of Empire* (Minneapolis: Fortress Press, 2008); and more broadly, Joerg Rieger, *Christ and Empire: From Paul to Postcolonial Times* (Minneapolis: Fortress Press, 2007).

18. It was the defining conclusion of German historical criticism in the nineteenth century that the prophetic texts were earlier than the Pentateuchal materials. That judgment is enshrined in the Documentary Hypothesis that has dominated scholarship with its evolutionary assumptions. Such a judgment readily and intentionally contradicts the claims of the canon itself. Scholarship is always left to adjudicate the complexity of the matter.

19. On the notion of "post-critical" in Paul Ricoeur that he dubbed "second naivete," see Mark I. Wallace, *The Second Naiveté: Barth, Ricoeur, and the New Yale Theology* (Macon: Mercer University Press, 1990).

20. See von Rad, *The Problem of the Hexateuch*, 1–78.

21. James Plastaras, *The God of Exodus* (Milwaukee: Bruce, 1966) provides the best summary of this movement in the exodus narrative.

22. For a clear summary of the Documentary Hypothesis, see John H. Hayes, *An Introduction to Old Testament Study* (Nashville: Abingdon, 1979), 155–97.

23. See Bernard M. Levinson, *Legal Revision and Religious Renewal in Ancient Israel* (Cambridge: Cambridge University Press, 2008).

24. H. H. Schmid, "Creation, Righteousness, and Salvation: 'Creation Theology' as the Broad Horizon of Biblical Theology," in *Creation in the Old Testament*, ed. Bernhard W. Anderson (Philadelphia: Fortress Press 1984), 102–17. See also Klaus Koch, "Is There a Doctrine of Retribution in the Old Testament?" in *Theodicy in the Old Testament*, James L. Crenshaw (Philadelphia: Fortress Press, 1983), 57–87; and Patrick D. Miller Jr., *Sin and Judgment in the Prophets: A Stylistic and Theological Analysis* (Chico: Scholars, 1982).

25. On the chapter, see Mark S. Smith, *The Priestly Vision of Genesis 1* (Minneapolis: Fortress Press, 2010).

26. See Walter Brueggemann, "'Impossibility' and Epistemology in the Faith Traditions of Abraham and Sarah [Genesis 18:1-15]," *ZAW* 94 (1982): 615–34.

27. See Aaron Wildavsky, *The Nursing Father: Moses as a Political Leader* (Tuscaloosa: University of Alabama Press, 1984).

28. For the thick and complex interrelatedness of Jewish and Christian textuality, see *Christianity in Jewish Terms*, ed. Tikva Frymer-Kensky, et al. (Boulder: Westview, 2000).

29. The reference to grandparents and grandchildren in Exodus 10:1-2 indicates a self-conscious intent in the narrative to provide a script for repeated performance.

30. I intentionally allude to the stunning study of Martha E. Nussbaum, *The Clash Within: Democracy, Religious Violence, and India's Future* (Cambridge: Belnap, 2007).

31. On the vexed historical questions, see William C. Dever, *What Did the Biblical Writers Know and When Did They Know It? What Archaeology Can Tell Us about the Reality of Ancient Israel* (Grand Rapids: Eerdmans, 2001).

32. For a thoughtful modernist attempt at the problem, see Douglas S. Earl, *The Joshua Delusion? Rethinking Genocide in the Bible* (Eugene: Cascade, 2010).

33. See Yosef Hayim Yerushalmi, *Zakhor: Jewish Hiatoey and Jewish Memory* (Seattle: University of Washington Press, 1982) and Michael A. Signor, ed., *Memory and History in Christianity and Judaism* (Notre Dame: University of Notre Dame, 2001).

34. See Walter Brueggemann, "The Recovering God of Hosea," *HBT* 3 no. 1 (2008): 5–20.

35. On the inherent violence of the national security state, see Chalmers Johnson, *Nemesis: The Last Days of the American Republic* (New York: Metropolitan, 2006).

36. See John Brueggemann, *Rich, Free, and Miserable: The Failure of Success in America* (New York: Rowman & Littlefield, 2010).

37. The deep claim of the gospel in this regard is evident in the teaching of Jesus in Luke 21:14-19. In verse 16 he says to his disciples who are to testify in public, "The will put some of you to death." The next verses, however, reverse field to affirm: "But not a hair of your head will perish" (v. 18). Clearly the happiness and safety of the gospel goes deeper than that imagined by most of us.

38. Robert Jay Lifton, *The Nazi Doctors: Medical Killing and the Psychology of Genocide* (New York: Basic, 1986), has chronicled the most atrocious "doubling" in the Nazi death camps. I do not suggest that our contemporary double-mindedness is anything like that practice. It is, however, something to ponder among us because the practice permits actions and policies about which we do not want to think.

39. Peter Berger, *The Social Construction of Reality: A Treatise in the Sociology of Knowledge* (Garden City: Doubleday, 1967), 157–58.

2. Prophetic Preaching as Sustained, Disciplined, Emancipated Proclamation

1. Walter Brueggemann, *The Prophetic Imagination*, 2nd ed. (Minneapolis: Fortress Press, 2001).

2. See Walter Brueggemann, *Solomon: Israel's Ironic Icon of Human Achievement* (Columbia: University of South Carolina Press, 2005).

3. On Moses and Martin Luther King, see Bruce Feiler, *America's Prophet: Moses and the American Story* (New York: William Morrow, 2009), 243–48 and passim.

4. Paul Ricoeur, "Biblical Hermeneutics," *Semeia* 4 (1975): 37–75. See Charles E. Reagan and David Stewart, eds., *The Philosophy of Paul Ricoeur: An Anthology of His Work* (Boston: Beacon, 1978), 239–45.

5. Walter Brueggemann, *Finally Comes the Poet: Daring Speech for Proclamation* (Minneapolis: Fortress Press, 1989), 3.

6. The notion of "the world in front of the text" is recurring in the writing of Paul Ricoeur. See, for example, James M. Edie, ed. *From Text to Action: Essays in Hermeneutics II* (Evanston: Northwestern University Press, 1991), 75–88.

7. William T. Cavanaugh, *Torture and Eucharist: Theology, Politics, and the Body of Christ* (Oxford: Blackwell, 1998).

8. Ibid., 278.

9. Ibid., 279.

10. Ibid.

11. Ibid.

12. See Robert R. Wilson, *Prophecy and Society in Ancient Israel* (Philadelphia: Fortress Press, 1980), 231–51. In our own time, we have examples of powerful persons who belatedly step outside the dominant narrative in a moment of self-recognition. Thus Robert McNamara seemed to learn very little from Vietnam but felt acute anguish over failed policies. McGeorge Bundy could belatedly admit that all the arrogant learning and posturing of his war architecture in Vietnam had been a disaster. And recently even Ben Bernancke could conclude that he had had over-confidence in the capacity of the market system to sustain itself. It is no wonder that now and then there are persons in powerful places who come to know better than the dominant narrative they are paid to sustain.

13. On these several images, see Walter Brueggemann, *Theology of the Old Testament: Testimony, Dispute, Advocacy* (Minneapolis: Fortress Press, 1997), 229–66.

14. See Feiler, *America's Prophet*, for a remarkable survey of the recurrence of the narrative. In even broader scope, see Michael Walzer, *Exodus and Revolution* (New York: Basic, 1985).

15. Michael Fishbane, *Sacred Attunement: a Jewish Theology* (Chicago: University of Chicago Press, 2008).

16. See Patrick D. Miller, *The Ten Commandments*, Interpretation (Louisville: Westminster John Knox, 2009).

17. See Brueggemann, *Solomon: Israel's Ironic Icon*, 142–44.

18. On new social possibility for Israel as "resurrection," see Jon D. Levenson, *Resurrection and the Restoration of Israel: The Ultimate Victory of the God of Life* (New Haven: Yale University Press, 2006).

19. See Jacqueline E. Lapsley, "Can These Bones Live? The Problem of the Moral Self in the Book of Ezekiel," *BZAW* 301 (Berlin: de Gruyter, 2000).

20. Ronald E. Clements, "Patterns in the Prophetic Canon," in *Canon and Authority: Essays in Old Testament Religion and Theology*, ed. George W. Coats and Burke O. Long (Philadelphia: Fortress Press, 1977), 49, 53.

21. Karl Barth, *The Word of God and the Word of Man* (New York: Harper, 1957), 45.

22. A stunning example of confidence in the dominant narrative was offered by Francis Fukuyama, *The End of History and the Last Man* (New York: Free, 1992). Fortunately, Fukuyama has since repudiated his outrageous thesis, though it continues to be held tenaciously in other quarters.

3. Loss Imagined as Divine Judgment

1. See Patrick D. Miller, *They Cried to the Lord: The Form and Theology of Biblical Prayer* (Minneapolis: Fortress Press, 1994), 55–134.

2. Emil L. Fackenheim, "New Hearts and the Old Covenant: On Some Possibilities of a Fraternal Jewish-Christian Reading of the Jewish Bible Today," in *The Divine Helmsman: Studies on God's Control of Human Events, Presented to Lou H. Silberman*, ed. James L. Crenshaw and Samuel Sandmel (New York: KTAV, 1980), 192–93.

3. Ibid., 199.

4. For an inventory of current remarkable study on the book of Lamentations, see Walter Brueggemann, *Out of Babylon* (Nashville: Abingdon, 2010), 46–48.

5. See Gunnar Myrdal, *An American Dilemma: The Negro Problem and Modern Democracy* (New Brunswick: Transaction, 1996). See also Fox Butterfield, *All God's Children: The Bosket Family and the American Tradition of Violence* (New York: Vintage, 2008).

6. *New York Times*, September 19, 2010, 1–13.

7. On the "if" of covenantal-Deuteronomic theology, see Walter Brueggemann, *Solomon: Israel's Ironic Icon of Human Achievement* (Columbia: University of South Carolina Press, 2005), 139–59.

8. See Moshe Weinfeld, *Social Justice in Ancient Israel and in the Ancient Near East* (Minneapolis: Fortress Press, 1995).

9. See Chalmers Johnson, *Blowback: The Cost and Consequences of American Empire* (New York: Holt, 2000).

10. On the contemporary connection, see Ellen F. Davis, *Scripture, Culture, and Agriculture: An Agrarian Reading of the Bible* (Cambridge: Cambridge University Press, 2009).

11. Hans Heinrich Schmid, *Gerechtigkeit als Weltordnung* (Tübingen: Mohr, 1968), and Rolf P. Knierim, *The Task of Old Testament Theology: Method and Cases* (Grand Rapids: Eerdmans, 1995), 171–224.

12. The best study of these Psalms is by Ben. C. Ollenburger, "Zion, the City of the Great King: A Theological Symbol of the Jerusalem Cult," *JSOT* 41 (Sheffield: JSOT, 1987). Ollenburger draws much more positive conclusions about these Psalms than I, but his study provides ready access to all the important issues.

13. Ronald E. Clements, "OT 'Woe' Oracles," *Anchor Bible Dictionary*, vol. 6 Si-Z, 945–46, reviews the way in which the "woe oracle" seems to be rooted in the sadness of funerary usage, but moves to prophetic invective that expresses intense anger: "It is possible, however, that nothing more was intended by the prophetic usage than to suggest, even perhaps vaguely, a funerary situation."

14. See Klaus Koch, "Is There a Doctrine of Retribution in the Old Testament?" in *Theodicy in the Old Testament*, ed. James L. Crenshaw (Philadelphia: Fortress Press, 1983), 57–87.

15. See Robert Jay Lifton, *The Nazi Doctors: Medical Killing and the Psychology of Genocide* (New York: Basic, 1986), 202–3 and passim. In a lighter but no less serious vein, we have this from "Reverend Billy," Bill Talen, *What Should I Do if Reverend Billy Is in My Store?* (New York: Free, 2003), 93–94:

> Dear Lord,
> We can't believe that bombing is called security.
> We can't believe that monopoly is called democracy.
> We can't believe that gasoline prices are called foreign policy. . . .
> We can't believe that racism is called crime fighting!
> We can't believe that sweatshops are called efficiency!
> We can't believe that a mall is called the neighborhood! . . .
> We can't believe that advertising is called free speech!
> We can't believe that love is called for sale! . . .
> George! Psst! Patriotism is not called shopping.
> Got that? Patriotism is not called shopping.
> Or better yet. George! Psst! This is God, George.
> I AM NOT THE MARKET.

16. Klaus Koch, "Is There a Doctrine of Retribution in the Old Testament?" in *Theodicy in the Old Testament*, ed. James L. Crenshaw (Philadelphia: Fortress Press, 1983), 57–87.

17. Ibid., 63.

18. Ibid., 65.

19. Ibid., 66, 69.

20. Patrick D. Miller, *Sin and Judgment in the Prophets: A Stylistic and Theological Analysis* (Chico: Scholars, 1982).

21. Ibid., 98, 102.

22. John Barton, *Understanding Old Testament Ethics: Approaches and Explorations* (Louisville: Westminster John Knox, 2003), 48–50.

23. Ibid., 117.

24. Terence E. Fretheim, *God and World in the Old Testament: A Relational Theology of Creation* (Nashville: Abingdon, 2005), 169.

25. Ibid., 179.

26. Ibid.

27. Abraham J. Heschel, *The Prophets* (New York: Harper & Row, 1962), 112.

28. YHWH's response to the disobedience of Israel that leads to the destruction of Jerusalem is not unlike the response of Nebuchadnezzar to the "fiery furnace" of Daniel 3:26-30. In that narrative, it is as though Nebuchadnezzar is helpless before the decree of punishment, so that the furnace cannot be averted; he is nonetheless relived when the young men are rescued by "their own God." So in prophetic discourse, it is as though YHWH cannot avert the punishment of Israel guaranteed by the inexorable structure of creation.

29. Fretheim, *God and the World*, 179.

30. Kenneth J. Doka, *Disenfranchised Grief: New Directions, Challenges, and Strategies for Practice* (Champaign: Research, 2002).

31. "Incarnate God, Immortal Love," in *The New Century Hymnal* (Cleveland: Pilgrim, 1995), 414.

4. A Lingering Place of Relinquishment

1. Abraham J. Heschel, *The Prophets* (New York: Harper & Row, 1962); see derivatively Kazoh Kitamori, *Theology of the Pain of God* (Eugene: Wipf & Stock, 1958, 2005). Jürgen Moltmann, *The Crucified God: The Cross of Christ as the Foundation and Criticism of Christian Theology* (New York: Harper & Row, 1974) has carried the insight of Heschel into the center of Christian theology.

2. See Patrick D. Miller, *They Cried to the Lord: The Form and Theology of Biblical Prayer* (Minneapolis: Fortress Press, 1994), 55–134.

3. Fredrik Lindstrom, *Suffering and Sin: Interpretations of Illness in the Individual Complaint Psalms,* Coniectanea Biblica Old Testament Series, 37 (Stockholm: Almqvist & Wiksell International, 1994), 185.

4. On the thickness and cruciality of this text for biblical theology, see Nathan C. Lane, *The Compassionate but Punishing God: A Canonical Analysis of Exodus 34:6-7* (Eugene: Pickwick, 2010).

5. Patrick D. Miller, *Sin and Judgment in the Prophets: A Stylistic and Theological Analysis* (Chico: Scholars, 1982).

6. See Jacqueline E. Lapsley, "Feeling Our Way: Love for God in Deuteronomy," *CBQ*, 65 (2003): 350–69.

7. J. Gerald Janzen, "Metaphor and Reality in Hosea 11," *Semeia* 24 (1982), 7–44.

8. Kitamori, *Theology of the Pain of God*, 151–67.

9. The same movement of divine inclination is reflected in the exilic text of Deuteronomy 4:24-31. At the outset, YHWH is "a devouring fire, a jealous God" (v. 24). At the end, YHWH is "a merciful God" (v. 31). The movement from the one to the other is accomplished "from there," that is, from exile (v. 29).

10. See Walter Brueggemann, "The 'Uncared For' Now Cared For (Jeremiah 30:12-17): A Methodological Consideration," *JBL* 104 (1985): 419–28.

11. Phyllis Trible, *God and the Rhetoric of Sexuality*, OBT (Philadelphia: Fortress Press, 1978), 31–59.

5. The Burst of Newness amid Waiting

1. See R. W. L. Moberly, *The Old Testament of the Old Testament: Patriarchal Narratives and Mosaic Yahwism*, OBT (Minneapolis: Fortress Press, 1992).

2. See David Noel Freedman, "Divine Commitment and Human Obligation," *Interpretation* 18 (1964), 419–31; David J. A. Clines, "The Theme of the Pentateuch," *JSOT* 10 (Sheffield: JSOT, 1978); and Claus Westermann, *The Promises to the Fathers: Studies on the Patriarchal Narratives* (Philadelphia: Fortress Press,1980).

3. Claus Westermann, *The Promises to the Fathers*, 60–61.

4. Karl Barth, *Church Dogmatics: The Doctrine of the Word of God, Second Half–Volume I* (Edinburgh: T & T Clark, 1956), 2.

5. Ibid.

6. Ibid., 3.

7. Eberhard Busch, *Drawn to Freedom: Christian Faith Today in Conversation with the Heidelberg Catechism* (Grand Rapids: Eerdmans, 2010), on the basis of the Heidelberg Catechism, has explored the freedom of God that stands over against Enlightenment notions of human autonomy.

8. On contrasting notions of the theological significance of thanks in the Old Testament, see Claus Westermann, *The Praises of God in the Psalms* (Richmond: Westminster John Knox, 1961), 27–30; and Harvey H. Guthrie Jr., *Theology as Thanksgiving: From Israel's Psalms to the Church's Eucharist* (New York: Seabury, 1981), 2–25.

9. Thus, for example, the desperate King Zedekiah can petition Jeremiah: Please enquire of the Lord on our behalf, for King Nebuchadrezzar of Babylon is making war against us; perhaps the Lord will perform a wonderful deed for us, as he has often done, and will make him withdraw from us" (Jer. 21:2).

10. Ronald E., Clements, *Old Testament Prophecy: From Oracles to Canon* (Louisville: Westminster John Knox, 1996).

11. See Walter Brueggemann, "A 'Characteristic' Reflection on What Comes Next (Jeremiah 32:16-44)," *JSOT* 229 (Sheffield: Sheffield Academic, 1996), 16–32.

12. See Rudolf Smend, *Die Bundesformel*, Theologische Studien 68; Zürich: EVS, 1963); and Rolf Rendtorff, *The Covenant Formula: An Exegetical and Theological Investigation* (Edinburgh: T. & T. Clark, 1998).

13. Jon D. Levenson, *Resurrection and the Restoration of Israel: The Ultimate Victory of the God of Life* (New Haven: Yale University Press, 2006), 95.

14. Ibid., 94.

15. Hans Heinrich Schmid, "Rechtfertigung als Schöpfungsgeschehen," *Rechtfertigung: Festschrift für Ernst Käsemann zum 70. Geburtstag*, ed. Johannes Friedrich, et al. (Göttingen: Vandenhoeck & Ruprecht, 1976), 403.

6. The Continuing Mandate

1. "God of the Prophets," *The New Century Hymnal* (Cleveland: Pilgrim 1995), 358. For biographical data on the author, see *The New Century Hymnal Companion* (Cleveland: Pilgrim, 1998), 390.

2. See Jon D. Levenson, *Resurrection and the Restoration of Israel: The Ultimate Victory of the God of Life* (New Haven: Yale University Press, 2006).

3. Alan E. Lewis, *Between Cross and Resurrection: A Theology of Holy Saturday* (Grand Rapids: Eerdmans, 2001).

4. See Marie Augusta Neal, *A Sociotheology of Letting Go: A First World Church Facing Third World People* (New York: Paulist, 1977).

5. I take the phrase "culture of interpretation" from Robert Alter who has so characterized emerging Judaism when the community on longer had significant political power but utilized its energy on the richness and complexity of its textual traditions. On the transfer from power to piety, see Jacob Neusner, *From Politics to Piety: The Emergence of Pharisaic Judaism* (Eugene: Wipf & Stock, 2003).

6. On true speech with transformative power, see James Boyd White, *Living Speech: Resisting the Empire of Force* (Princeton: Princeton University Press, 2006).

7. Emmanuel Levinas, *Totality and Infinity: An Essay on Exteriority* (Pittsburgh: Duquesne University Press, 1969).

8. On transformative rhetoric that defies the rhetoric of "order," see John D. O'Banion, *Reorienting Rhetoric: The Dialectic of List and Story* (University Park: Pennsylvania State University Press, 1992), who contrasts the rhetoric of list and story.

9. Martha C. Nussbaum, *The Clash Within: Democracy, Religious Violence, and India's Future* (Cambridge: Harvard University Press, 2007).

10. Ibid., 15.

11. Samuel P. Huntington, *The Coming Clash of Civilizations and the Remaking of World Order* (New York: Simon & Schuster, 2003).

12. Nussbaum, *The Clash Within*, 337.

13. Lawrence Thornton, *Imagining Argentina* (New York: Doubleday, 1987). I have found this book through the citation of William Cavanaugh, *Torture and Eucharist* (Oxford: Blackwell, 1998).

14. Thornton, *Imagining Argentina*, 98–99.

15. Ibid., 108.

16. Ibid., 136–37.

17. Ibid., 65.

18. Ibid., 99.

19. See Walter Brueggemann, *Out of Babylon* (Nashville: Abingdon, 2010).

20. Michael Walzer, *Exodus and Revolution* (New York: Basic, 1985), 149.